Rimbaud

Rimbaud

The Double Life of a Rebel

Edmund White

Atlantic Books
LONDON

First published in the United States of America in 2008 by
Atlas and Co.

First published in hardback in Great Britain in 2009 by
Atlantic Books, an imprint of Grove Atlantic Ltd.

10 9 8 7 6 5 4 3 2 1

A CIP catalogue record for this book is available from the
British Library.

ISBN: 978 1 84354 971 0

Interior design by Yoshiki Waterhouse
Typesetting by Sara E. Stemen

Printed in Great Britain by MPG Books Ltd, Bodmin

Atlantic Books
An imprint of Grove Atlantic Ltd
Ormond House
26–27 Boswell Street
London
WC1N 3JZ

www.atlantic-books.co.uk

To Carol Rigolot

"The novel of living together as two men"
– Verlaine

When I was sixteen, in 1956, I discovered Rimbaud. I was a boarding student at Cranbrook, a boys' school outside Detroit, and lights out was at ten. But I would creep out of my room and go to the toilets, where there was a dim overhead light, and sit on the seat for so long that my legs would go numb. Outside, the wind was driving the snow into high white silencing drifts; inside, the dormitory was eerily quiet. I would read and read again Rimbaud's poems. Even though I had won a local prize in French, Rimbaud's vocabulary and grammar were too difficult for me and I was always peeking from the left page of the French original to the right page of the 1952 English translation by Louise Varèse. Buoyed up by the sensual delirium of the long poem "The Drunken Boat," I would float off into daydreams of exotic climes.

As an unhappy gay adolescent, stifled by boredom and sexual frustration and paralyzed by self-hatred, I longed to run away to New York and make my mark as a writer; I identified completely with Rimbaud's desires to be free, to be published, to be sexual, to go to Paris. All I lacked was his courage. And genius. I crammed all my homework into the afternoons, when most of the other boys were playing sports. That way I was free during the two-hour compulsory study hall in the evening to work on my novel. I wrote one novel, then a second. My mother, ever indulgent, asked her secretary to type them up from my neat, handwritten pages. My idea was that I would send them off to a New York publisher, have them accepted, make a fortune—and flee. I'd cast aside both my parental households (my parents were divorced), liberate myself from their money, quit my school—and move to New York! I imagined an older man would fall in love with me and do everything for me.

For some reason, I never sent off my manuscripts. Maybe I didn't know where to mail them; after all, I'd never met a published writer, nor did such a fabulous creature seem to inhabit our Midwestern world, any more than a unicorn might suddenly gallop past my dorm windows. Or maybe I was afraid that my book would be accepted, that it would be published, that I would have to live out all my fantasies—and the notion of answered prayers I found even more alarming than a continuation of my dependence and frustration. After all, in Rimbaud's nineteenth-century Catholic village, a homosexual might have been a sinner or a criminal, but in the Freudian 1950s in America, he was sick and in urgent need of treatment. A sinner might insist he wanted to be a Prodigal Son, a criminal might want to be irredeemable, but no one could fight for the right to be sick.

I found the Rimbaud myth to be at once puzzling and exciting. In a slim volume about Rimbaud by Wallace Fowlie, published by New Directions in 1946, just a decade previously, I read these fascinating words: "A relationship between two poets of the same sex, even if there is a physical basis, may provide an intensive intellectual comradeship and stimulation. Homosexuality, in its highest sense, is founded on intellectualism. It represents fundamentally an aesthetic conception of love, in which the beauty of a young man seeks the wisdom of an older man, and in which wisdom contemplates beauty." Fowlie then went on to trot out Plato and the ideas of the *Symposium*. Only recently did I discover that Fowlie was both a champion of modernism and a Catholic who remained celibate for forty-five years—and went on to write a last book in the 1990s about Rimbaud and Jim Morrison, lead singer of The Doors!

These ideas about homosexuality "in its highest sense" were heady indeed, "even" if physical—and rhymed with the life of the great Russian dancer Vaslav Nijinsky, and his tragic affair with his impresario lover, Sergei Diaghilev, the founder of the Ballets Russes. My mother had given me a biography of Nijinsky just before I discovered Rimbaud, and there, too, I read,

> Diaghilev's boundless admiration for Nijinsky the dancer was even overshadowed by his passionate love for Vaslav himself. They were inseparable. The moments, in a similar mutual relationship, of dissatisfaction and ennui that came to others, never came to them, as they were so intensely interested in the same work. To make Sergei Pavlovich happy was no sacrifice to Vaslav. And Diaghilev crushed

any idea of resistance, which might have come up in the young man's mind, by the familiar tales of the Greeks, of Michelangelo and Leonardo, whose creative lives depended on the same intimacy as their own.

To read that the two men "were one in private life" thrilled me, just as I was half-convinced by Diaghilev's argument that heterosexuality was an animal necessity for breeding, "but that love between the same sex, even if the persons involved are quite ordinary, because of the very similarity of their natures and the absence of a presupposed difference, is creative and artistic." Oddly enough, this strange and questionable homage to homosexuality had been written by Nijinsky's wife Romola (not so odd, perhaps, since Romola, as I only recently learned, was a lesbian).

The only problem in the case of Rimbaud, however, was that the boy, Rimbaud, dominated the older poet, Verlaine. Rimbaud was the top, the "Infernal Bridegroom," and Verlaine, ten years older and married, was the passive "Foolish Virgin." For a while I referred to this book as "Rimbaud: Teen Top." To be sure, Rimbaud enjoyed shocking his older straight male friends by claiming otherwise. He once said about Verlaine in the presence of Alphonse Daudet, the macho Provençal novelist, "He can satisfy himself on me as much as he likes. But he wants me to practice on him! Not on your life! He's far too filthy. And he's got horrible skin."

Not only did Rimbaud control and harass and terrorize Verlaine in the bedroom, but he also sought to prevail in their work, despite Verlaine's established reputation and publishing history. Rimbaud was the exalted revolutionary who thought poetry must break with tradition and usher in a whole new era of human history. As Paul Valéry declared, "Before Rimbaud all literature was written in the language of common sense."

If Rimbaud was the most experimental poet of his day, someone who in the four short years of his career managed to have three utterly different styles, then Verlaine was much more a lyric voice, someone whose superb verses were close to the delicate, rhyming patterns of song (indeed, Debussy set them to music), a poet of melancholy and shadows, of a fragile and intensely personal Catholicism, and of the springtime of love. In 1890, looking back at his entire production, Verlaine said that the constants of his style included "a free form of versification...frequent alliteration, something like assonance in the body of the verse, rhymes more rare than rich, the exact word sometimes avoided on purpose or nearly. At the same time, the content sad and designed to be that way...." In this statement Verlaine accurately emphasized the sadness and the strict formality of his distinctive verse.

In the little Fowlie book, no longer than this one, I learned that Rimbaud had wooed Verlaine away from his wife; that they had fled to London, that there they had almost died of starvation; that they had associated in England with the former Communards; the anarchists who had tried unsuccessfully in 1871 to establish Paris as a free city-state and been forced to flee to England. Verlaine, fearing he'd made a mistake in abandoning his wife and baby son, rushed back to the Continent, where a distraught Rimbaud joined him. In Brussels they had another fight. Verlaine shot Rimbaud through the wrist—and the older man was given a two-year prison sentence. In prison Verlaine returned to the Catholic faith, wrote pious poetry—but when he was freed he ran back to Rimbaud's side, rosary in hand, just as later Oscar Wilde would be imprisoned for homosexuality, repent, write a pious confession and, after serving his two-year sentence, seek out Lord Alfred Douglas, the cause of his downfall.

Rimbaud, I read, left behind an important body of work but renounced his career at age nineteen, went off to Africa, earned money as a gunrunner, became ill, and died an early death. Verlaine, a genius and a drunk, would stagger on for several years more; he would write a biographical sketch of Rimbaud, see his works into print, and do whatever he could to promote the fame of his lost love. Rimbaud's literary career lasted four years and he died at age thirty-seven; Verlaine published over a period of some thirty years and he died at age fifty-one. Verlaine was a survivor, though he was also a buffoon, lurching back and forth from men to women, from wine to absinthe, from hospital to prison to gutter, all the while turning out pure musical poems that made him the spiritual leader of the Symbolists. While still in school, I read a novel by the turn-of-the-century writer Anatole France called *The Red Lily*, in which a character, based on Verlaine, wrote his best poems on cigarette paper and smoked them in front of appalled admirers.

The contrast between Rimbaud, the short-tempered, willful hellion, prompt to renounce one career after another until he ended up sick and despondent and virtually friendless, and Verlaine, the subtle, self-pitying equivocator, quick to yield even to his worst impulses—this contrast fascinated me. In my early twenties I wrote a play about Rimbaud and Verlaine, which made the rounds but was never put on; as one producer explained to me, "Either Rimbaud is a genius, to whom everything is permitted, or he's a brat. Genius is impossible to establish on the stage, so by default he comes off as an intolerable troublemaker and ingrate."

Wallace Fowlie's meditation on Rimbaud's life and the longer 1936 biography by Enid Starkie were all I had to go on in my high-school days, but these traces of the Rimbaud-meteor were enough to give me hope—as a desperate, self-hating homosexual, as an aspiring writer, as a sissy-rebel. I, too, wanted to reach out to older writers in New York and have them extend a welcoming hand, as Verlaine had welcomed the unknown Rimbaud (and sent him the money for a train ticket to Paris). I, too, wanted to escape the ennui of my petit-bourgeois world and embrace bohemia. I, too, wanted to forego years of apprenticeship and shoot to the artistic top as a prodigy, not a drudge. I, too, wanted to make men leave their wives and run off with me.

The worst thing I may ever have done in my life was to denounce a teacher at Cranbrook for smoking marijuana. He was eventually fired, and he was subjected for years to the scrutiny of the FBI, whom the school authorities had tipped off. What I never mentioned to them was that I had had sex with this very teacher—and had denounced him for smoking marijuana the same day. My self-hatred, my desire to have a trapdoor beside the bed where I could toss the "evidence" of my sickness and sin—certainly these played a part in my disgusting behavior, as did my resolve not to be tempted again. And perhaps I was bitter and nursing my disappointment that my teacher wanted to get off with me but didn't love me (he was married). Now, all these years later, I ask myself whether Rimbaud's "satanic" example might not have been the decisive influence on my deplorable behavior.

Arthur Rimbaud certainly didn't look like the devil. Like a fallen angel, perhaps, with his thick, untamable hair that he grew to his shoulders when he was sixteen and his sky-blue eyes that come out nearly white in the photographs of the day, his small features and determined, unsmiling mouth. Verlaine called him "an angel in exile." The slight asymmetry of the center dip in the cupid's bow of his upper lip is one of those intriguing flaws in an otherwise perfect face that makes the viewer catch his breath. I suppose it's right up there with James Dean's bashful-boyish-guilty way of lowering his head and looking up at us through his eyebrows with a smile. Verlaine later spoke of Rimbaud's "cruel light blue eyes" and his "strong red mouth with the bitter fold in it—mysticism and sensuality in spades."

Rimbaud was born on October 20, 1854, in the town of Charleville in the northeast corner of France called the Ardennes, near the Belgian border—best known to foreigners as the region where the disastrous Battle of the Bulge was fought during World War II. Prophetically, Rimbaud was born in his parents' apartment above a bookshop. Charleville was one of those French rural towns with imposing public buildings from the seventeenth century gathered around a cobblestoned Ducal Square, several church spires, dismal little neighborhoods of a uniform grayness, the muddy streets empty and the shutters closed except on market days—a town, yes, but never out of earshot of roosters crowing and the rumble of horse-drawn carts full of hay. The whole town dozed beside a nearly motionless branch of the Meuse River flowing beside a massive stone mill from the seventeenth century that looked like a bell tower.

"Rimbaud" is derived from *ribaud*, an old French word that is related to *ribald* in English and means "prostitute," hardly a proper name for the pious family of Catholic farmers on his mother's side, but perhaps more appropriate to the bearer of the name, his father, a dashing captain in the army, a tailor's son who at age thirty-eight married a dour peasant woman of twenty-seven for her solid character and handsome dowry and her prospects of inheriting more. He seems to have spent very little time with Vitalie Cuif, but when he was with her he kept busy, since during each visit she conceived another child. First came Arthur's older brother, Frédéric. Then, less than a year later, Arthur was born, baptized Jean Nicholas Arthur Rimbaud. When the baby's birth was registered at the town hall, one of the witnesses was the bookseller downstairs, Prosper Letellier. Six months after Arthur's birth, his father was sent off to fight in the Crimea. He came back briefly during the summer of 1856 and, like clockwork, nine months later a little girl, named Vitalie after her mother, was born, but she died within a month.

No matter. Less than a year later a second daughter, also named Vitalie, came into the world. In 1859 Madame Rimbaud paid her husband a visit at his garrison, and nine months later she gave birth to a fourth and final child, Rimbaud's beloved sister Isabelle, who would be with him when he died and who would do much to promote his posthumous fame, though she also devoted extraordinary energy to cleaning up his image.

Five children in six years of marriage (four survived) was quick work, but it seems that Captain Rimbaud didn't much like children and didn't get along with his stern and bigoted wife. One day in 1860, he left Charleville to join his regiment and never returned. Arthur was six. His mother was someone guided at every moment by a strong sense of duty and self-discipline. Her mother had died when she was still a child, and little orphaned Vitalie had run her father's household from an early age. Though she was determined to rise into the middle class and to push her children even higher, she herself had worked in the fields when she was growing up. Nevertheless she could read and write and had a high regard for education. No one had ever seen her smile. She subscribed to rigidly conservative principles and once became enraged when she saw little Arthur reading Victor Hugo's *Les Misérables*, a novel we'd consider fit for the whole family. She boxed Arthur's ears and denounced the teacher who'd lent him the book. After all, the novel was on the Catholic index and Madame Rimbaud took her faith seriously.

She admired ceaseless labor and probably could barely tolerate what she considered to be her husband's doodling. He had been stationed for several years in Algeria, at that time a French colony, and there he wrote all sorts of very long unpublished books—a collection of jokes in Arabic, an annotated and translated Koran, a compendium of high points in military oratory, ancient and modern, reports on all the evils that befell his regiment, everything from locust attacks to dealings with two-faced Arab diplomats. None of these copious writings still exists (probably Madame Rimbaud destroyed her husband's belongings after his death); but we know that Arthur Rimbaud studied his father's works in Arabic as he attempted to learn the language.

Curiously, given that Africa was to be Arthur's destiny, Madame Rimbaud's brother got into trouble with the law, ran off, and spent years fighting in Algeria. When he returned to the Ardennes, he was so tan that everyone dubbed him "the African." If Madame Rimbaud was strict, it was possibly because she secretly feared that her children would turn out badly—want to travel, drink, and live the life of wastrels.

Arthur seems to have harbored erotic memories (or fantasies) of his father. When he was seventeen and living in Paris, he wrote a series of parodies of other poets, including the popular bourgeois rhymester François Coppée, whom he despised. In this jocular context, Rimbaud felt free to write:

I daydreamed about my father sometimes;
In the evening, a card game and off-color jokes,
The man from next door, and I seated off to one side,
    things seen...

For a father can be disturbing!—and the things
  dreamed up!
His knee, nudging me sometimes; his trousers
Whose fly my finger wanted to explore—oh no!
In order to touch one of my dad's bits—big, black
  and hard—
He whose hairy hand had rocked my cradle!

Her older son, Frédéric, was a blue-eyed boy, amiable and even cheerful, a slow learner but a predictable and easygoing person. He would finish three years of high school, join the army, and see some action (thereby exempting his younger brother, Arthur, from needing to serve). Eventually Frédéric would sell newspapers, go back into the army for another five years and attain the rank of sergeant, work on a farm and then become a tramway conductor, marry, have children, and die in his sixties—a life like millions of others. In the army Frédéric picked up a broad, drawn-out Provençal accent; when Rimbaud later recounted to him some of his strange adventures as a vagabond, Frédéric drawled, "You disgust me-e-e...."

Soon after her husband abandoned her and their children, Madame Rimbaud announced that she was a "widow"; indeed, she always signed her letters "Madame Rimbaud—Widow." She was thirty-five when he left her. The family came down in the world—they moved to a back street where the other families were poor. Although Madame Rimbaud forbade her children to play with the ragamuffin neighbors, Arthur was fascinated by them. In his early poem, "The Seven-Year Old Poets," he recalls:

The only children he spent time with were
Skinny and bare-headed, their eyes lackluster,
Who hid their yellow fingers black with mud
Under their old rags stinking with diarrhea
While they conversed with the sweetness of idiots.…

Often enough Madame Rimbaud has been portrayed as an unfeeling, closed-minded woman, but her extant letters, written late in life, reveal her to have been resourceful, pious, and loyal, if undeniably tight-buttoned. In her letters to her daughter she announces, "Since there is no more religion there is no more honesty," and she seems to be implying that her daughter's own husband may have pocketed a money order intended for his wife. Typically she will close a letter saying, "My daughter, pray to God and do your duty in all things." Or at the end of the year she will write, "I'm not going to wish you a happy new year, that's useless, actions are all that count." When her daughter was going to marry a writer who'd lived for years in Paris, Madame Rimbaud wrote to Stéphane Mallarmé himself, the high priest of the Symbolist cult, asking for a character reference. Mallarmé sent one, highly favorable, responding no doubt out of respect to the mother of Rimbaud, by then deceased.

Madame Rimbaud's weirdest remark in her letters to her daughter Isabelle is, "At the moment when I prepared to write you, some soldiers here passed by, which gave me a very powerful feeling as I remembered your father with whom I would have been happy if I'd not had certain children who made me suffer so much."

It seems unlikely that she is referring to all her children or children in general; certainly she is not singling out Isabelle, who was always respectful and obedient. She may have meant the first Vitalie, who died as an infant and cast her mother into a terrible state of despair. She may have meant Arthur, the genius from hell, the one she loved the most and who gave her endless trouble as a teenager (though late in life he turned out all right). She probably meant her older son, Frédéric, who was the slowest boy in school and grew up to be a tramway conductor, a scheming wretch who even threatened to blackmail his own brother.

Though Arthur had become a rebellious teenager, as a boy he had been scarily good. As he writes in "Seven-Year-Old Poets":

And the Mother, closing the exercise book,
Went away satisfied and very proud, without noticing
In his blue eyes and on his forehead so prominent
  with genius,
The child's soul giving in to revulsion.
All day long he sweats with obedience, very
Intelligent; however, certain fidgets and looks
Seem to prove he's guilty of being a nasty hypocrite.
In the dark corridors with their mildewed curtains
He sticks out his tongue as he walks by, plants both
  fists
Against his groin and squeezes his eyes shut till he
  sees stars.

Later in the poem, Rimbaud speaks of his fascination with men strolling home in the evening after work. He says clearly that while he was made to read the family Bible with its cabbage-green borders, he didn't love God—just these men. Later he would talk about his attraction to the "unredeemable convict whom the penitentiary will lock up forever. I'd visit the inns and furnished rooms he would have sacralized by staying there. Through his eyes I saw the blue sky and the flourishing work of the countryside; I picked up the scent of his fatal presence in the cities. He was stronger than a saint, more sensible than a traveler— and he, he alone!, is the only one to prove he is famous and in the right." In two different poems, Rimbaud writes about going to the outhouse and daydreaming there about sex and escape. Like the young criminal-poet Jean Genet, born a half century later but brought up in a similar village, the young Rimbaud believed the outhouse was the one place of retreat and reverie. Both boys, scholarly and obedient as children, secretly admired prisoners. Indeed, though both Rimbaud and Genet went on to turn into delinquents and wild boys, both of them started off as model students and superior scholars. Rimbaud had a mother, if not a father, but he thought of himself as an orphan, and his first published poem was a sentimental ballad about orphaned children, toddlers who've been abandoned by careless relatives in a freezing house, their only toys the beaded funeral wreaths of their deceased mother. Rimbaud and his brother celebrated their first communion together, and a year later Rimbaud, unbeknownst to his teachers and family members, sent off to the Prince Imperial in Paris (Napoleon III's son) an ode in Latin, sixty lines long, celebrating the imperial boy's first communion (the Prince's preceptor wrote back a nice note, though he chided Rimbaud for a few mistakes in the classical language).

Rimbaud's scholastic excellence was incontestable. There on the printed program at the end of what would be middle school in America is a list of Rimbaud's prizes—first in History and Geography, first in "academic competition," first in Latin composition, first in Greek and so on. He was the best student Charleville had seen in many years. Legend has it that during the six-hour regional exams in 1869, Rimbaud conspicuously daydreamed with his head down on his desk for the first three hours—then sped through the entire workload in the remaining time and won all the honors. No wonder a teacher reported that the student was "small and timid" and "a little stilted and ingratiating. His fingernails were clean, his exercise books spotless, his homework amazingly correct, his grades above reproach." The teacher said he was one of those "perfect little monsters" built to win contests. The image remains indelible of Madame Rimbaud on Sunday morning marching to church with her two silent, obedient sons and her two silent, obedient daughters walking behind her, all turned out impeccably.

Some of Rimbaud's first poems are about village life. While still a kid, he had already become resolutely anti-bourgeois in the great tradition of French bourgeois authors. He once scrawled in a school notebook, invoking the names of two of the bloodiest (and long-dead) participants in the French Revolution, "Marat and Robespierre, the young await you!" At the age of fifteen, he had suddenly turned into a caricaturist (he even drew some pretty good caricatures of local types in his notebooks). In "To Music" he speaks of a military band playing in the square next to the train station during the height of summer. He makes fun of "the club of retired grocers who rake the sand with their knobbed canes" and of "the fat office-workers who drag their big ladies along" while the narrator, the "I" of the poem, follows the young girls and studies their "white necks embroidered with stray locks of hair" and hopes to catch a glimpse of their boots and stockings. In a less satirical poem, called "Novel," Rimbaud develops in a light, carefree manner the theme of the flirtatious girl and the amorous lad: "You're scarcely serious when you're seventeen." In one stanza he writes (inventing a verb based on Robinson Crusoe):

> The heart goes madly Robinsonning through novels
> When, in the pale light of street lamps,
> A young miss with charming airs floats by
> Shadowed by her father's fearful detachable collar…

Perhaps Rimbaud was influenced by Verlaine who, in his first poem, "Monsieur Prudhomme" (1863), had written similar words:

> He is serious: he is the mayor and father of the family,
> His false collar swallows up his ear…

Rimbaud even speculates about his own mother's physical loneliness and stifled sense of longing in the wake of her husband's abandonment. In "Memory" he writes about "Madame" who holds herself too upright in the field beside the Meuse River as her children stretch out in the grass and read their red leather-bound book. Then, dramatizing the scene, Rimbaud imagines:

> Alas, like a thousand white angels vanishing above the road,
> He disappears through the mountains! And she, cold and black,
> Runs! Yes, runs after the departure of the man!

In the next stanza, Rimbaud pictures his mother longing for sturdy young arms and thinking of a gold April moon illuminating the marriage bed. She recalls the ripe germinating evenings of August, as if passing from lovemaking to the full implications of pregnancy, the inevitable outcome of her couplings with her husband. Toward the end of the poem, the writer remembers his frustration as a child—his arms were too short to reach out to the flowers; he could not touch either the troubling yellow one nor the blue one, the flower melting into the ash-colored water. The reader cannot help but think of the annoying mother and the rapidly receding father, both beyond their son's grasp.

Arthur and his older brother, Frédéric, were opposites. Whereas Arthur was always at the top of his class, his brother was always among the last. At first they attended the Rossat Institution, a run-down but prestigious academy. When Arthur was eleven their mother transferred her sons to the local private *collège*, or secondary school. Arthur amused himself by drawing pictures of his teachers, but this silent rebellion was the only ruffle in an otherwise exemplary comportment. The principal was soon devoted to Arthur, who he was certain would vindicate the reputation of his school in the regional scholastic competitions. The principal told his staff to let young Arthur read anything he liked—no censorship for his star pupil.

Rimbaud, however, was hanging around the bookstore and (since he couldn't afford to buy expensive magazines or books) reading there the latest poetry coming out of Paris in the annual anthology *Contemporary Parnassus*. There Rimbaud immersed himself in the work of a fairly new school of poetry, the Parnassians, the apostles of Art for Art's Sake, who subscribed to Théophile Gautier's statement, "Only that which serves no end is beautiful; everything useful is ugly." Though they were heirs to Romanticism, they reproached the Romantics for their sentimentality and for taking political positions (for or against democracy, for or against Napoleon). Unlike the Romantics, the Parnassians emphasized a return to the literature of antiquity and prized impersonality and the icy perfection of form.

As in the case of all literary movements, not all or even most of its adherents truly followed its principles. For Rimbaud the Parnassians meant an exposure to the idea of the avant-garde, which for him was crucial. When the only poets you've ever read in your little sleepy village, cut off from the great world, write in Latin and Greek and have been dead for two thousand years, the notion that contemporary poetry (even the staid, classicizing Parnassian poetry) is in a state of permanent revolution and that only the new is worthwhile affected Rimbaud profoundly. He himself had just published a poem in Latin in the *Monitor of Secondary Instruction*, an imitation of Horace in which Phoebus, the sun god, declares prophetically, "You will be a poet."

In the Parnassian anthology, the poet he admired most was Paul Verlaine, the man who would eventually become his lover, savior, and downfall. During this first literary exposure, Rimbaud was influenced by Verlaine's poems. When Rimbaud wrote letters to his elders about the mission of poetry, he would evoke passages from Verlaine about the robustness of ancient Greek poetry— and cite even the same names of classical poets of the past.

On January 2, 1870, the fifteen-year-old Rimbaud published his first poem in French in a respectable wide-circulation journal, the *Review for Everyone* (*La Revue pour tous*). The poem, called "The New Year's Day Gifts for the Orphans," is a skillfully done but sentimental ballad about little children awakening on the holiday morning to discover that their mother is dead, the grate is cold, and they've been abandoned to their fate by their father. Every heartstring is plucked. The predominating influence is clearly Victor Hugo (who in "Things Seen One Spring Day" writes: "The four children wept, and their mother was dead").

It was as if the simple act of publication awakened the prince from his slumbers and plunged him into what would henceforth be an action-packed life. Yeats said that the writer must choose the life or the work; Rimbaud ended up choosing both.

Rimbaud's new teacher at school was Georges Izambard, a twenty-year-old poet who had been hired as a professor of rhetoric and who right away alarmed his provincial superiors by attacking Voltaire's moth-eaten verse dramas in class, little realizing that Voltaire was not only a despised atheist and free-thinker but also the defender of France's greatness (for Voltaire there were only four great epochs—those of Pericles, the emperor Augustus, the Medici, and Louis XIV). To attack this second Voltaire was to question France's royal destiny—and for such a mistake Izambard was shadowed during the rest of his career by a questionable reputation. In the frightfully narrow-minded world of the French provinces, Izambard had already blotted his copybook during his previous job by attending the annual firemen's ball and dancing with two ladies of questionable repute. He was also hard of hearing, which made it difficult to maintain classroom discipline (several of his students at Charleville were also older than he). His students nicknamed him "Zanzibar," which perhaps he didn't hear. (Oddly enough, the island of Zanzibar later became the mythic destination of Rimbaud's life, which he never reached.) Izambard left teaching soon thereafter to become a researcher, and even dabbled unsuccessfully for a while with the earliest applications of x-rays and moving pictures.

Something about this outspoken professor must have appealed to the young Rimbaud—and once he learned of it, the boy was also strongly attracted to Izambard's library. Izambard had a large collection of all the most recent books of French poetry and literary journals, as well as many of the classics, and was willing to lend these volumes to the eager student. In a small town, and in an era before the prevalence of public libraries, the problem of just getting one's hands on books could be nearly insurmountable.

Izambard had been brought up as a solitary, bookish child, raised by three maiden ladies after his mother died in a cholera epidemic when he was a baby. The young professor was at first suspicious of Rimbaud, the locally famous, prize test-taker, but soon he discovered that the boy was just as isolated as he, and even more enamored of poetry. Izambard began to give private lessons in academic subjects to Rimbaud (under his tutelage, Rimbaud wrote Latin verses on the assigned contest topic, "Sancho Panza Addresses His Donkey"), and he introduced him to Rabelais, Rousseau, and the great fifteenth-century thief-vagabond-poet François Villon.

Villon and Rabelais were vestiges of a nearly effaced tradition in French letters that was bawdy and outrageous, as well as rife with an extensive, wild, and invented vocabulary—everything that had been wiped out by the purist French Academy in the seventeenth century.

Perhaps this renewed Renaissance influence led Rimbaud to become both erotic (with his own especially pitiless contempt for the body) and linguistically inventive (*Robinsonning* as a verb). Later, apparently, Verlaine would counsel Rimbaud to return to a more restrained, humble vocabulary (which can, paradoxically, be more expressive), and Rimbaud, intermittently, would follow his advice.

Madame Rimbaud was grateful for the free tutoring Izambard provided her son but suspicious of the books he passed along. In fact the Rimbaud family continued well into the twentieth century, long after Rimbaud's death, to blame Izambard for having introduced the worm into the apple and misled their precious genius into the ways of vice and extravagance. In one sense they might have been right, but Izambard's responsibility was at most indirect; the teacher presented the precocious boy to other local book-lovers and bohemians, and Rimbaud discovered that in this arty, adult world he was at home at last. Through Izambard, Rimbaud also glimpsed the teeming world of letters and publishing that was flourishing far away in Paris—and the boy was more eager than ever to flee his town.

Before Izambard, Rimbaud had had a few friends among his classmates, notably one called Ernest Delahaye, who later became a Parisian literary personality. Delahaye became his most faithful and copious correspondent. The son of a local shopkeeper, Delahaye ended up as an official in the department of public instruction. He wrote numerous reminiscences about Rimbaud—and about Paul Verlaine, who later became another lifelong friend. Delahaye tended to glorify Rimbaud and to play down the abrasive aspects of his personality, but he does provide many anecdotes and direct quotations from Rimbaud's conversation—a record that would otherwise be nearly blank. It was Delahaye, for instance, who bore witness to Rimbaud's taciturnity; according to Delahaye, Rimbaud could go two days without speaking at all. At the same time, if Rimbaud felt relaxed and confident he could become very jolly and talkative (everyone attests to his strange little dry chuckle).

Of course, as a teenager Rimbaud was most infamous for his oaths and swear words. Delahaye remarked on Rimbaud's gift for picking up accents. He could imitate anyone—which helped him no doubt to acquire foreign languages, Delahaye asserted. In his memoirs Delahaye recalled many of Rimbaud's comments. He remembered that when the Emperor lost a battle, Rimbaud exclaimed, "Napoleon III deserves a convict ship." When he was fifteen he told Delahaye that an orphan or wild child was better off than they were: "Brand new, clean, without any principles, without notions—since everything they teach us is false!—and free, free of everything." As early as October 1870, Rimbaud told his friend that he was going to write in a new, made-up language: "To create a poetic language that speaks to all the senses, I'll take words from scholarly and technical vocabularies, from foreign languages, wherever I can...."

But it was Izambard, not Delahaye, who recognized Rimbaud's split personality. As he wrote, talking about the mother's nefarious influence, "There was the Rimbaud of the school, sealed-off and reticent, who appeared even then still to be under the iron fist that ruled him; the exact opposite was the Rimbaud of our discussions, who gave free rein to his inner self in a sort of intellectual exuberance.[...]Rimbaud himself later understood this doubling of his personality when he wrote me: 'I is another person.'"

Under the stimulating influence of his new teacher, Rimbaud began to write a poem almost daily. First there was his invocation, "Ophelia" ("Here for more than a thousand years the sad Ophelia / Has floated, a white ghost, down the long black river"), a carefully sculpted imitation of the poetic models the boy had been studying, especially the poems of the arch-Parnassian, Théodore de Banville, who sponsored young poets and had been an on-again, off-again friend of Baudelaire's. In the following weeks Rimbaud dashed off a "medieval" poem in Old French, another ballad about skeletons dancing on the gibbet (inspired by Banville)—and, most notably, a sensual poem about desire and the urge to travel, just eight lines long and called "Sensation":

On a blue summer evening I shall go down the path
And, brushed by wheat, walk on the fine grass.
Dreaming along, I'll feel the coolness under my feet
And bathe my bare head in the poetic wind.

I won't speak, I will not even think,
But infinite love will geyser up in my soul,
And I'll go far, far away, like a gypsy
Into the wilds—as happy as if I were with a woman.

Just as he'd once sent a Latin poem to the Prince Imperial, he now wrote a letter in his most beautiful calligraphy to Banville, who was not only a poet but also a playwright, drama critic, and cultural journalist and who was tied to all the leading literary lights of the day. Rimbaud included his poem on Ophelia (originally prompted by a Latin assignment) and several others, and wrote:

> Two years from now, or perhaps in a year, I shall be in Paris...I shall be a Parnassian!—I feel there is something in me...that wishes to rise...—I swear, dear Master, that I shall always adore the two goddesses, Muse and Liberty.
>
> Please do not turn up your nose at these lines.... You would make me mad with joy and hope if, dear Master, you could obtain for the poem 'Credo in unam' a small place among the Parnassians....I would appear in the last series of Le Parnasse: it would be the poets' Creed!...Oh mad Ambition!

He ended his letter by writing in the best oracular style:

> I am unknown; what does it matter? Poets are brothers. These lines believe; they love; they hope; and that is all. Dear Master, help me up a little. I am young. Hold out your hand to me.

Although Rimbaud claimed in the letter to be seventeen, he was really just fifteen and a half. Maybe if Banville had liked boys and not girls he would have responded more positively; in any event he did not take any of the poems. What is apparent is that Rimbaud, even before he was sixteen, was reaching out to the great world—eager to escape his town, no longer committed to his studies and a profession, drunk with the idea of becoming a poet among poets.

The poem he calls "Credo in unam" ("I believe in one," from the Catholic credo, as in "one holy church," or in this case "one goddess") he later renamed "Sun and Flesh," a better title since it is about a pre-Christian worship of nature. It contains the lines:

> I regret the time when the world's sap,
> The chattering river water, the blood of green trees
> Created a universe in the great god Pan's veins.

Later he apostrophizes Venus (and rejects Christ with pagan blasphemy):

> I believe in You! I believe in You! Divine Mother!
> Aphrodite of the Seas! Oh, life is bitter
> Ever since another god has harnessed us to his cross!
> But it's in you, in you, O Venus, I believe!
> Yes, Man is weak and ugly and doubt assails him,
> And he wears clothes because he is no longer chaste....

The poem is a riot of nymphs, cupids, fauns and Olympian bulls and timorous swans—all hailing from the regretted, waning world of antique sensuality.

Suddenly Rimbaud's suffocating world was blown apart. In July 1870, Imperial France declared war on Prussia. Napoleon III went into battle against the Prussians and on September 2 was captured with one hundred thousand of his men in Sedan, a town just twelve miles away in the Ardennes. The defeat at Sedan brought the Second Empire to a humiliating close, allowed the Prussians to pour into France and occupy it, and introduced a chaotic period that ended only with the founding of the Third Republic.

While these exciting events were occurring, Rimbaud was also exploding. On August 6 he was awarded several academic prizes, but he was already way beyond their power to interest him. He was now a writer among writers, though his beloved Izambard (touchy, hard of hearing, pipe-smoking) had left Charleville on July 24 to spend the rest of the summer break with his "aunts" (the ladies who'd raised him) in Douai far to the west. Rimbaud was beside himself with restlessness. He let his hair grow, and soon it reached halfway down his back. He looked like a Romantic—a pocket version of a Romantic, because he was still just five foot three inches tall (though by the end of 1871 he would be five foot eight, considered tall at the time).

He wrote Izambard: "You're lucky you don't have to live in Charleville anymore!" Though Rimbaud complained of the sight of grocers in uniform, what really outraged him was the lack of newspapers and books: "The post has stopped sending things to booksellers. Paris is really treating us shabbily: not a single new book!"

On August 29, 1870, Rimbaud sold some books and with the few francs he earned made his first of several escapes from home. The direct train route from Charleville to Paris had been cut off by Prussian soldiers. Rimbaud headed north toward Belgium, changed trains at Charleroi, and arrived on August 31 at the Gare du Nord in Paris with a ticket that was valid for a much shorter distance. Penniless and friendless, he was arrested as a vagabond for traveling without a proper ticket and put into the Mazas Prison near the Gare de Lyon. His clothes were fumigated and his carefully nursed long hair was cut. He claimed he had to defend his virtue against the sexual assaults of the other inmates—a bizarre collection of petty criminals, spies, and anarchists. Two days after Rimbaud's arrest, Napoleon III capitulated, and two days after that the Empire collapsed—it was a strange moment to be in the hands of government officials. To add to the oddness, just a few months previously a peasant, Jean-Baptiste Troppmann, had been tried for the brutal murder in 1869 of an entire family of eight, the Kincks. (Both Troppmann and one of the little Kincks showed up in Rimbaud's occasional comic verse.) Troppmann had been imprisoned at the Mazas awaiting his execution. His trial had been one of the most sensational in French history—and his execution turned into a gigantic crowd-pleaser, a true circus attracting hundreds of spectators who bought tickets for the best "seats." The crowd had gathered well in advance; one man fell from a tree and died the night before the execution. After Troppmann was guillotined, two men rushed forward to dip their handkerchiefs in his blood.

Rimbaud, who'd dreamed of freedom and the bohemian life, was now frantic to get out of prison. He wrote letters to his mother, to the appropriate imperial official (who was very soon to be out of a job), to the police chief in Charleville—and to Izambard. He demanded that his teacher come to Paris, spring him from jail and pay off his train ticket debt. He also requested that Izambard write Madame Rimbaud "to console her." And finally he added, "If you are able to get me out, you will take me to Douai with you." Izambard followed his instructions to the letter and soon Rimbaud was installed with the three Gindre sisters, the ladies who'd raised Izambard. The ladies doted on Rimbaud—and since the country was occupied by enemy troops, there was no question at the moment of his returning to Charleville.

His mother thought otherwise. She dashed off a firm letter to Izambard insisting that her son not pass another night in Douai. Rimbaud, however, made no move. He and Izambard drilled with the local militia, using broomsticks because no guns were available. Rimbaud wrote a letter to the mayor of Douai complaining of the lack of weapons, though he failed to garner enough signatures from local citizens to validate the petition.

While Madame Rimbaud clamored for her Arthur to return, the boy luxuriated in the attentions of the three maiden ladies. Perhaps he was thinking of them when he wrote a poem about two "charming" older sisters who search a boy's head for lice (vermin he might have picked up in prison):

> Silence; and their soft electric fingers
> Rustle through his dull drowsiness
> And crush lice under their royal thumbs.

This poem, "The Lice-Seekers," shocked his contemporaries. It was one of the few Rimbaud poems singled out in the early years of his career, and it was always cited as an example of how outrageous the poet was. He had carried Baudelaire's "nostalgia for filth" to new heights, it was said. There is something perverse and disturbing in the poem, but it derives not from the lice but from the heavy, slow "caresses" administered to the child (for he is just a baby in the poem) by these women with their "delicate" fingers, "bewitching and terrible," and the sound of their lips being licked. The baby begins to sink into the sweet lethargy of passivity, which Rimbaud compares to the eerie, queasily sliding sound made by the glass harmonica (not a mouth organ but the keyboard instrument that Mozart had written a composition for).

The spoiled little Rimbaud also exulted in the many books in the Gindre sisters' library. Years later, Izambard could remember his brilliant pupil repeating again and again a passage he had discovered in the essays of Montaigne: "The poet, seated on the tripod of the Muses, furiously spits out everything that enters his mouth, acting like a fountain gargoyle, and out of him flow things of all different sorts, contrary substances in an uneven flow." This idea of a grotesque, varied, and artesian inspiration would haunt the young poet, the image of the writer as simple conduit for conflicting, heterodox forces welling up out of him. Through Izambard, Rimbaud was introduced to Paul Demeny, a published poet a few years older than Rimbaud, and for him Rimbaud copied out all the poems he'd written in the preceding year.

Since Madame Rimbaud could no longer be pacified, Arthur returned to Charleville, accompanied by Izambard, who visited the town briefly mainly in order to remove his books to the safety of Douai (the region of Charleville was already occupied by the Prussians). Rimbaud fell back on the company of his friend, Ernest Delahaye, and the two boys walked constantly back and forth from one neighboring village to another, talking literature, smoking homemade cigarettes, bored witless. Their school had not reopened and the whole region was under Prussian control. Everyone looked at his or her neighbor as a potential spy. The two boys, indifferent to the goings-on around them, read Victor Hugo's poetry out loud to one another and wrote articles for a new newspaper that a local photographer was starting up (the Prussians quickly suppressed it).

Soon after he returned to his mother's house, Rimbaud took off again. He was so overwhelmed by ennui that as he later wrote Izambard, "I'm dying, I'm dissolving in all that is platitudinous, evil, gloomy. What can I do— I'm stubbornly devoted to adoring free freedom—am I tugging at your heartstrings yet?" Grim as his first visit to Paris had been, even in prison he had paradoxically learned a taste for "free freedom." This horror of a settled existence, this deep aversion to a sedentary life, would obsess him till the end of his days.

Rimbaud was crossing a line. He was no longer just a runaway scamp but, at least in his mother's eyes, a juvenile delinquent. When he showed up after a long and leisurely stroll through Belgium and back down to Douai, his mother ordered Izambard to turn him over to the police, who would take charge of the young criminal and force him to come home, in chains if necessary.

During the trip through Belgium to Douai, Rimbaud had written some of his most cheerful poems, true songs of the open road—and poems that are decidedly heterosexual. For those modern readers who like to think that sexual orientation is straight or gay and always neatly categorized, Rimbaud is worrisomely hard to classify. Though he would feel a strong, destructive passion for Paul Verlaine, his other interests before and afterward were mostly with women. Nor were these heterosexual adventures a form of cool, rational "therapy," a conscious effort to "go straight," as we would put it. Both Rimbaud and Verlaine wrote bawdy poems about sex with women, and Verlaine, at least, can only affectionately be described as a "dirty old man." He was up for anything and ended up with not one but two mistresses, who squabbled fiercely over him.

Rimbaud would come to believe that love must be reinvented, that heterosexuality almost always devolved into spiritless marriage, and that women must learn to be men's comrades, not their wives. This ethical rejection of marriage would dominate the thinking of *A Season in Hell*, but when he abandoned his writing altogether, he would also push aside the ideas it embodied.

Before Rimbaud met Verlaine his poems were all heterosexual—and not just routinely so but quick with finely observed details of village soubrettes, coy maidens, saucy waitresses, shy girls. In a typical poem of this period, "Three Kisses," he writes:

> Nearly naked and seated on my big
> Chair, she joins her hands
> And taps the floor in contented ecstasy
> With little feet so fine, so fine

A month or so later he was writing a poem to a certain Nina who laughs at him, brutal with giddiness, while he ravishes her and drinks in her taste of raspberry and strawberry. When he was fifteen and sixteen, Rimbaud— small and pretty as a girl himself—could not write ten verses without devoting at least one to a girl's laugh, leg, open mouth, or scent.

Rimbaud at sixteen going on seventeen during his leisurely hike to Douai was rhapsodic with the excitement of flirting with Belgian barmaids and inventing his rhymes while he strode across the countryside, versifying in a continuous rhythmic murmur, just as one might say the rosary. In "The Sly One" he writes:

In the brown dining room scented with the odor
Of varnish and fruit, I contentedly dig into
A Belgian concoction of some sort
As I spread out in my giant chair.

While I eat I listen to the clock—I'm happy and
   silent.
The kitchen door suddenly bangs open
And the servant girl rushes in with (I don't know
   why)
Her scarf half untied and her hair piled up prettily.

With a trembling little finger she strokes her cheek,
As downy as a pink and white peach,
And pouts with her childish lips.
She stands near me and casually fiddles with the
   plates.
Then, out of the blue to persuade me to kiss her, she
   says
Softly: "Feel this—My cheek has caught a terrible
   cold!"

Many of the poems written during these months (with
Rimbaud one must speak of months instead of years,
since he changed at such a rapid rate) are about village
coquettes, the simpering, tormenting kind who wink
and then put on virginal airs. In a poem written at the
same time, "At the Green Cabaret, Five in the Evening,"
Rimbaud again talks about stretching out his legs under
the green table while a big-breasted waitress ("As for
that gal, no kiss would ever scare her off!") serves him

buttered bread, slices of pink and white ham that have cooled down and been flavored with a bit of garlic—and she gives him a big stein of foaming beer lit up by the setting sun. The hungry young vagabond seems torn between the ham and the big-breasted girl. And notice that for the little poet all chairs seem to be "giant." And just as the sly girl in these verses points out to him where her cheek has caught cold, in yet another sonnet the poet rides with a girl in a pink wagon and she lowers her head to him and says that she feels a spider running across her skin and she wants him to catch it…slowly.

These poems may not be the heart-wrenching or delirious or icy masterpieces that Rimbaud would soon compose, but they are charming and sensual and full of a joie de vivre we don't usually associate with him. For once he's not lampooning bourgeois hypocrites or Tartuffe-like priests; nor is he envisioning a coldly utopian future nor bitterly regretting the past. For once he is fully alive to the simple pleasures of the flesh, of play, of freedom, and of food. Perhaps the best of the lot, "My Bohemia," vividly renders the thrill of being a teenager on the road. With his "fists stuffed in pockets full of holes," he marches along and dreams of "splendid love." His pants have a big rip in them, his usual "shelter was nothing but the Big Dipper / —And the stars up above rustled softly like a woman's skirt." He continues:

I listened to them as I sat next to the road
During those fine September evenings when I felt
    drops

Of dew on my forehead like drops of strong wine;
Where, reeling off rhymes as the shadows turned
    strange,
I strummed the laces of my run-down shoes
Like harp strings, one foot jammed against my heart!

There is something delightfully cartoonish and indelible in this picture of the boy "playing" his shoelaces—all the pleasures of art, daydreaming, masturbation, and freedom coming together in a single electrifying image.

At this moment in late October 1870, just as he was turning seventeen, Rimbaud began a life given over to vagabondage, to restless traveling, while seeking adventure or profit or simple employment, perhaps, but always driven to go on, go on. He was always flying down the roads on his "soles of wind" (*semelles de vent*). His remaining twenty years would see him constantly in motion; a biographer of Rimbaud could fill his pages with nothing but his ceaseless comings and goings, his itineraries.

During this journey Rimbaud stayed with classmates, stopping off in Brussels and making his way back down to Douai, where he installed himself again with the amiable Gindre sisters. Izambard himself was out combing the countryside in search of his former student. Mission unaccomplished, he returned to Douai only to discover the poet being coddled by the three maiden ladies. This time Madame Rimbaud was categorical: the truant should be handed over to the police, who would accompany him back to Charleville. Rimbaud bade farewell to his teacher, little knowing they would never see each other again.

Rimbaud went peacefully, after copying out all his new poems for his new friend Demeny. One of the poems, "The Sleeper in the Valley," is a perfect sonnet very much in the manner of Victor Hugo. It describes a young soldier asleep, "head uncovered. Mouth open / And his nape bathing in the cool blue watercress." He's smiling like a sick child, his feet planted among the lilies:

The sweet smells don't make his nose wrinkle,
He sleeps in the sun, hand on chest,
Peaceful. He has two red holes through his right side.

Back in Charleville with his stern, unforgiving mother, Rimbaud had no freedom and nothing to do. His mother announced that she was going to send him off the following semester to a tough boarding school. His own school was still closed because of the Prussian invasion (Prussian soldiers were constantly patrolling the streets). For once Rimbaud wrote little, except letters to Izambard full of complaints of boredom. The Prussians bombarded the neighboring town of Mézières, killed a number of citizens, and destroyed the grocery shop belonging to his friend Delahaye's family. Fortunately, the Delahayes themselves had taken refuge in the country.

It might have been at this time that Rimbaud wrote (under a pseudonymn) a short, satirical sketch about Bismarck that he published in a Charleville newspaper. In the sketch, Rimbaud imagines the German general hnched over a map of France, looking longingly at the black dot that symbolizes the much-coveted Paris.

Bismarck is smoking a pipe. He falls asleep on the pipe and map and badly burns his big nose. He is forced to attend the royal Prussian sauerkraut dinner with a black stub of a missing nose. It's all a bit schoolboyish, but it is a discovery (the text had not been seen for 138 years).

By February 1871, the Prussians were at the gates of Paris. The French had declared a Republic after Napoleon III was defeated in battle, but it was still a weak, disorganized power. The Prussians under Bismarck demanded of the new, defeated government a huge indemnity of five billion francs and the return of Alsace and the eastern part of Lorraine. On February 26, 1871, the newly elected French leader Adolphe Thiers signed the punitive and humiliating Treaty of Versailles. A month earlier, the Prussian army had occupied Paris, but its control of the still-armed, restless and rebellious city remained only partial.

From March 26 to May 30, Paris rebelled against the Prussians (and against the government of Thiers, established in nearby Versailles) and created the Paris Commune, the first elected Communist government in history. The Communards quickly declared an international city open to workers from every country throughout the world. They dissolved the official status of the Catholic Church (and its right to government subsidies). They closed down pawnshops as institutions oppressive to the poor. They even pulled down one of Napoleon Bonaparte's proudest symbols, the column in the Place Vendôme, which sixty years earlier had been assembled from the melted-down cannons of France's defeated enemies. Thiers's French soldiers, in collusion with the Prussians, laid siege to Paris, finally breached its defenses, and slaughtered tens of thousands of the Communards.

Rimbaud was aware of all these dramatic events as they were beginning to build up, and he was eager to trade in the enforced boredom of Charleville for the history-making excitement of Paris. Toward the end of February 1871, Rimbaud sold his watch and headed off for Paris. There he stumbled into a city that was starving to death—the people had even been reduced to eating the animals in the zoo. The boy slept in coal barges, bought a smoked herring he made suffice as food for several days, visited all the bookshops again and again and examined the newest volumes, mostly about the war. The cold was severe. Rimbaud remembered the name of a caricaturist and let himself into his studio, where he fell asleep. The shocked artist, André Gill, awakened the boy and told him he couldn't stay there but did give him ten francs.

Cold, dirty, and hungry, the friendless Rimbaud walked days and days the 150 miles back to his mother's house. Once again he was stymied and defeated. On March 10 he arrived in Charleville, skinny and wracked with a cough. No sooner was he home than the Commune was declared in Paris. Rimbaud sympathized with the Communards. Like them, he was violently anticlerical. Like them, he mocked the authorities, the bourgeoisie, the deposed monarch. Many of his poems written in 1870 and 1871 reveal how subversive he could be. "Venus Anadyomène" describes the goddess of love with a body that smells bad, shoulder blades that stick out and, on her rump, a huge boil. "The Dazzling Victory at Saarbrück" mocks the Emperor's defeat at the hands of the Prussian enemy and ridicules all the toadies who once surrounded him. One poem after another makes fun of priests—shown shitting over their chamber pots or hypocritically lusting after girls. Rimbaud laments the lot of the poor who worship at the church in their benighted fashion while indifferent rich women dip their long yellow fingers into holy water. He writes of the young people whose natural lust is blasted by the curse of puritanical religion ("Christ, O Christ, eternal thief of the will"). Rimbaud pictures virgins sitting on the toilet in the outhouse, horny priests stripping naked, pure young men driven mad by religion. In a long prose work of this period, "A Heart Under a Cassock: A Seminarian's Innermost Thoughts," he writes a mocking but curiously touching story about an eighteen-year-old monk-in-training who falls in love with a girl, Timothée Labinette. She ridicules him because his feet smell. She gives him a clean pair of socks, which he puts on and refuses to change until he dies and enters paradise. Meanwhile he composes sincere but inadvertently heretical verses to the Pregnant Virgin, which make his classmates roar with laughter.

When Rimbaud heard about the Commune, he marched through the streets of Charleville with glittering eyes and called out, "That's it! Order has been banished." At last the hateful, smug bourgeoisie was getting its comeuppance, so long overdue after the first Revolution of 1789 and the later ones of 1830 and 1848. Now, the

Commune of 1871 seemed to promise the end to middle-class life as it had become in the nineteenth century. Rimbaud told a stoneworker he met, "All workers must rise up in solidarity." (Later that summer Rimbaud would write something called "Project for a Communist Constitution," which has been lost.)

In April his school was no longer being commandeered as a hospital for the war-wounded. It had been fixed up enough to be usable again as a place of learning and was about to reopen. Madame Rimbaud, disgusted with her long-haired layabout of a son—a lout who'd turned blasphemous, disrespectful, and jeering against all forms of moral and political order—gave young Arthur an ultimatum: either he returned to school or found a job.

Very briefly Rimbaud started working as a journalist, but five days later the paper, *Le Progrès des Ardennes*, was suspended by the occupying authorities. Faced with an impending return to school, Rimbaud succumbed again to the lure of Paris and the Commune. Sometime toward the end of April he entered the beleaguered city on foot; when he passed through the gates of Paris, he announced he'd just walked all the way from the Ardennes and was penniless. The soldiers cheered him and passed the hat and gave the proceeds to the astonished and grateful boy.

Perhaps initially Rimbaud enjoyed the edgy, carnival atmosphere of the contested city. And maybe it was there that he learned from older anarchists to be surly, dirty, and rude—a final twist he gave to his natural antibourgeois manners and morals. Paris in crisis was acting as a magnet for thousands of runaway young men and women; if a hundred thousand middle-class people had fled the city, then their places had been quickly filled by all the young wastrels of the crumbling empire. Rimbaud was writing poems (now lost) called "Death of Paris" and "The Lovers of Paris." In one extant fragment—as pierced with exclamation points as the body of St. Sebastian is wounded with arrows—Rimbaud calls for an end to all republics, emperors, regiments, colonists, and subjugated peoples! He commands Europe, Asia, and America to vanish! He orders industrialists, princes, and senators all to perish!

Enid Starkie in her hugely influential biography, published in 1937, proposed that Rimbaud was raped by soldiers while in Paris and that this terrifying event was the major turning point in his life. She was inspired by the speculations in a French biography by a Colonel Simon Godchot that had appeared shortly before. There is no first-hand evidence of a rape, but Starkie—whose biography is wonderfully readable and highly novelistic—bases her entire argument on "The Tortured Heart" (*"Le Coeur Supplicié"*), a strange and opaque poem that could be interpreted in many different ways. Piling up speculation on supposition, Starkie writes:

> Up to now Rimbaud had remained, in spite of his intellectual maturity, a child in experience, who had been carefully sheltered from the ugly side of life.[...]It is quite obvious from the poems he had written before April 1871 that he had as yet had no actual experience and singularly little

sexual curiosity; even his imagination had remained innocent and childish. The only person to have stirred his emotions was Izambard. [...] At sixteen, when he went to Paris, he still looked like a girl, with his small stature, his fresh complexion and his reddish-gold wavy hair. It is probable that he then received his first initiation into sex and in so brutal and unexpected a manner that he was startled and outraged, and that his whole nature recoiled from it with fascinated disgust. But though this experience brought him shock and revulsion so great that he fled from Paris to hide his wound at home, there was more to it than mere recoil. It was not solely an unpleasant experience which had disgusted him and against which he could stiffen himself; it was one that did not leave him indifferent, nor his senses untouched. It was a sudden and blinding revelation of what sex really was, of what it could do to him, and it showed him how false had been all his imagined emotions. ... He was never the same again.

Starkie's next paragraph begins with the sentence, "This experience was probably the most significant ever in Rimbaud's life, and had he been personally psycho-analyzed, not merely his work, psychologists would have seen in it the turning point of his development, and would have traced to it the source of much of his later maladjustment and distress."

Of course, Starkie was a convinced and ingenious

Freudian, looking for the trauma that would act as the decisive moment in Rimbaud's subsequent life. That moment, naturally, must be tied to sex—and the trauma it caused was exacerbated by the fact that "unconsciously" Rimbaud had enjoyed it.

Everything here is pure invention. How do we know that he enjoyed being raped? First there is no evidence that rape ever occurred. He could have been beaten up or robbed or attacked by soldiers without being raped. It seems unlikely that in a city like Paris—famous for its prostitutes and at that moment overwhelmed with anarchists, male and female—a group of soldiers would have felt the need to ravage a boy in the barracks or would have had any excuse for doing so in front of one another. Prisoners or sailors on shipboard, or soldiers in the field, long deprived of the company of women, might sexually assault a boy *faute de mieux*, but a rabble army in Paris? Probably not. To go from a putative rape to the conclusion that Rimbaud enjoyed it (I would argue that the number of men or women who actually enjoy being raped is very small indeed), and to conclude that this hidden pleasure shaped the rest of his life, seems highly illogical. Of course, if you start out with the Freudian idea that homosexuality itself is a sign of "maladjustment and distress," then the diagnostician must work back from that troubling condition to some triggering trauma. Few biographers today would subscribe to such a theory, but Starkie's scenario has been vastly influential in Rimbaud narratives. It finds an odd equivalent myth in the idea that T. E. Lawrence was raped by Arabs and liked it. And how strange that Starkie thought that rape revealed what "sex really was." The finesse with which she jumps from "it was probable" that he was raped to the conclusion that this was indubitably the key experience of his life is very skillful indeed as a piece of rhetoric. A lot of Starkie's argumentation is based on double negatives ("not solely an unpleasant experience"; "did not leave him indifferent"), which quickly give way to such dramatic affirmations as "the turning point."

The poem that inspired all this speculation is called variously "The Tortured Heart," "The Heart of a Clown," and "The Stolen Heart." It reads:

My sad heart drools on the prow,
My heart soaked in tobacco spit.
They spit streams of liquid,
My sad heart drools on the prow.

Fully erect and terribly martial,
Their insults have degraded it.
Along the tiller you see painted frescoes
Fully erect and terribly martial.
O waves chanting magic spells,
Take my heart and let it be washed clean.
Fully erect and terribly martial
Their insults have degraded it.

When they'll have spit out their tobacco
What will you do then, O stolen heart?
There will be Dionysian hiccups

When they'll have spit out their tobacco.
My stomach will be turning over
Even if I swallow my nausea
When they'll have spit out their tobacco
What will you do then, O stolen heart?

The poem is clearly disturbing. Yet when Izambard received it in the mail, and found it unsettling and refused to take it seriously, he should have paid more attention to the almost tremulous care with which Rimbaud had submitted it to him, telling his former teacher that "it does not mean nothing" ("*Ça ne veut pas rien dire*"). Izambard's cold reception of the poem alienated Rimbaud, who was obviously setting great store by it. Although Izambard praised its "magisterial finish" and "headlong energy," nevertheless he couldn't see what it meant and accused it of being full of "scatological images." Worse, Izambard dashed off a parody of Rimbaud's poem, which drove the young poet into a rage. Essentially it was the end of their friendship. The young poet valued his creation either as a formal invention or as a veiled confession, or both, while Izambard's parody missed the point. They lived in a rough-and-tumble bohemian world of heavy teasing and ready banter (the same hand-to-mouth, easygoing, impious student sphere that Henri Murger had described in his Montmartre sketches, *Scènes de la vie de Bohèm*, the source of Puccini's *La Bohème*), yet Rimbaud obviously felt vulnerable and deeply resented Izambard's insensitivity. Years later, Izambard would say, "He was, I think, a homosexual—yet despite my invincible disgust for that breed he himself did not disgust me because I saw through to the noble motives he was obeying."

Izambard's failure of sensitivity was all the more striking because the poem accompanied a serious letter that became a key document in the Rimbaud legend, especially when he rewrote it and enlarged it and sent it to Demeny. This missive, known as "The Seer's Letter," is one of the foundations of modern poetry. In his shorter letter to Izambard he had written, "*Je est un autre*" ("I is someone else"), which meant that in the act of introspection we objectify the self, we experience our self as if it belongs to another person. In the act of introspection there is an observer and there is an observed—and the observed half of the ego feels distant, alien. In writing to Demeny, Rimbaud added, "This much seems obvious to me: I am present at the explosion of my thought. I watch and I listen to it. I wave the baton; the symphony murmurs from its depths or comes leaping onto the stage."

The letter goes on to rant against the poetry of the past, which has become mildewed. "Let the new writers denounce their ancestors! We're at home in the present and we have plenty of time." In the past, writers were bureaucrats, functionaries. "An author, a creator, a poet— that sort of man has never existed!" In other words, we are about to witness the birth of the true poet, who will exist for the first time in history. This premonition of the dawn of a new era sounds strangely like the predictions made by the German philosopher Friedrich Nietzsche twenty years later.

In order to become a true poet, Rimbaud wrote, the writer must turn himself into a seer. "The Poet becomes a seer through a long, immense and carefully reasoned disordering of all the senses." The poet must subject himself to a self-instigated torture; he must undergo all the agonies of love, suffering, and madness. "He needs all his faith, all his superhuman force, and he will become the great sick man, the great criminal, the great cursed sinner—and the supreme Wise Man, since he'll have reached the Unknown."

Rimbaud then added a poem, "My Little Love-Birds," filled with odd words, heavy irony, grotesque images, and stomach-turning descriptions. After the insertion of the poem, the letter continues with an examination of the role of language. The poet must steal fire from the heavens. He is responsible for humanity, even for other animals; he must make the things he invents appeal to our taste, touch, and hearing; if the things he brings over from the beyond already have a form, then he gives them a form, but if they are nebulous he must leave them unformed.

The time has come for a universal language. This language will speak directly from one soul to another. The poet will define how much of the unknown will awaken in the universal soul during his lifetime. He will give even more: in the sentences that follow, Rimbaud seems to be extolling some future utopia where poetry will outstrip thought, where it will represent a materialist future. The future of poetry and the future of the world seem to be intertwined. Again and again Rimbaud cries out for the new—new words, new forms, a new society. Women will become the poets of the future and will introduce men to new ideas that are "strange, unfathomable, repulsive, delicious."

Finally Rimbaud reviews the Romantic poets of the recent past (including Victor Hugo, to whom he owes so much) and finds them all wanting for one reason or another. Hugo had irritated him in particular by attempting to reconcile the Communards to the Thiers government at Versailles. Only Baudelaire "is the first seer, king of the poets, a true god." Baudelaire's only fault was that he lived in a falsely elegant, arty milieu and failed to invent brand-new forms. In the list of Rimbaud's immediate contemporaries, Paul Verlaine is the only living poet to get a favorable mention.

The "Letter of the Seer" is remarkable because it makes a clean break with the past and calls for a radical reinvention of poetry. The poet is a seer who achieves his visionary powers by disordering his senses through alcohol, drugs, madness, disease, and crime. Just as Baudelaire had spoken of the virtues of intoxication, which permit the individual to merge with the world around him and with universal humanity, in the same way Rimbaud ascribed the poet's supernatural lucidity to everything that broke down the dulling habits of perception. And although the wording of Rimbaud's letter is exalted and "spiritual," it invokes a materialist idea of progress, progress being the byword of late nineteenth-century progressives like Rimbaud—all of whom had such confidence in mechanical inventions, industry, and science.

Rimbaud's unusual homage to women and especially women poets is characteristic of the illuminist authors he was immersing himself in, all of whom subscribed to an idealist feminism. The prolific female novelist George Sand, the beautiful South American but French-speaking intellectual Flora Tristan, and the frail, tubercular love poet Louisa Siefert from Lyons—these were some of the women of his epoch whom Rimbaud undoubtedly had in mind.

The "Letter of the Seer" is not a Romantic rejection of society, of the new, of democracy. Though Rimbaud was increasingly bizarre in his slovenliness, his jerky movements, and his outrageous insults, in his approach to art he was anything but an isolated dandy or a brutish iconoclast. He had embraced the democratic ideals of the Commune, and he dreamed of a future in which progress would ensure happiness, and science and art would collaborate. He sounds at times like Baudelaire, especially in his contempt for bourgeois prudishness and his love of what is urban, new, and artificial. But unlike Baudelaire, he does not want to retreat into a crepuscular world of pitch-perfect sonnets. Instead, Rimbaud sees the poet more as an annotator, a midwife to new sensations, someone who can jot down virtually anything that his senses detect and perceive.

This objective poetry of pure sensation is an impulse that Rimbaud most perfectly embodied in his famous sonnet "Vowels," written in the summer of 1871. Here he riffs on the five vowels and attributes a color and a story to each. Critics have seen in these associations proof of his interest in alchemy (a subject he studied seriously in the Charleville library) or in "synesthesia," the substitution of one sense for another, a theory that

Baudelaire had advanced in his art writing of the 1840s, which held that hearing, for instance, might appear to the poet as colored forms. Incidentally, the novelist Vladimir Nabokov would much later claim that he experienced a link between sounds and colors, *audition colorée*, as the French call it. But as Antoine Adam, one of the most careful Rimbaud commentators, argues, the particular associations may have more to do with the way the letters look, especially as they might have been written by a schoolboy of Rimbaud's time. Thus the letter *e* was written as a Greek epsilon by Rimbaud, and if an epsilon is turned on its side it does look like the frozen "lances of proud glaciers" that the poet describes, just as the letter *I* when tilted resembles a pair of compressed lips. (One ingenious critic even turned the five vowels into a map of the female body.) Perhaps no theory works exactly, but the poem could exist only in the world of poetic correspondences and mystic links first proposed by Baudelaire. Or maybe the five letters are something like the elements of the Word that God pronounced in order to create the world. And Rimbaud was perfectly ready to compare himself to the demiurge.

Back in Charleville and the moral and political vacuum created by the Commune, Rimbaud became a sophisticated idler. He scrawled obscenities on the walls of his town ("Shit on God" was a favorite). He debated literature and politics with a few of the local intellectuals at the Café de l'Univers across from the train station or at the Café Dutherme in the Place Ducale. Mostly he sat alone, furiously puffing on his pipe, scowling and writing.

He was still awaiting a letter from Demeny about his poetical theories; when one came it was unsatisfactory. Madame Rimbaud—whom he referred to in English as "the Mother," just as he called Charleville by its English equivalent, "Charles Town"—had laid down the law. Once again, either Rimbaud was to return to school or start earning his living; she would no longer support a dirty, belligerent ne'er-do-well. Rimbaud wrote once more to the well-known Parnassian poet Théodore de Banville, a man in his late forties who had been a friend of Baudelaire's and was an intimate of the other most talented poet of the day, Stéphane Mallarmé. Banville was subject to nervous breakdowns, but despite his occasional disarray he produced an abundant output, eventually collected after his death in 1891 in a total of nineteen volumes. As one of the founders of the Parnassian movement, he was known for the restraint and classical decorum of his verse. Now Rimbaud seemed deliberately set on offending him. His letter to the older man sounded fawning and insincere, and in the first quatrain of his own enclosed verse Rimbaud referred to lilies as "enemas of ecstasy." A few lines down he spoke of "a sea bird's excrement," and of violets that were the "sugary spittle of black nymphs."

That poem, "What People Say to the Poet about Flowers," is a strange contraption that might easily have irritated Banville, though it was meant to appeal to him (many of Banville's own rhymes and images are echoed by Rimbaud as complimentary allusions). If the poem is read carefully, it turns out to be an attack made by an old bourgeois philistine on a weak-kneed Romantic poet who keeps gushing on about lilies when he should be addressing serious matters—that is, serious according to the old bourgeois—such as guano and potassium mines. The modern world, the old man is saying, has no use for the flowery nonsense of the past. The strategies of this poem—with its deeply embedded and unsympathetic old man and its fool of a young poet who resembles Banville a bit too closely—seem calculated to rub Banville entirely the wrong way. Perhaps Rimbaud had built up such a head of belligerent steam that even when he wanted to court someone he couldn't help but offend.

In Charleville the young poet, still imbued with the revolutionary atmosphere of the Commune, treated most of his fellow townsmen with contempt—although he did unbend slightly for an older gay man of Falstaffian girth, Charles Bretagne. The son of a government official, Bretagne himself was a very minor clerk in charge of "indirect taxation" at a sugar refinery, but his job was not demanding and in his free time he read incessantly and engaged in playful banter at the local café. There he became intrigued with Rimbaud and invited him to a musical evening in his rooms and lent him books about alchemy, mysticism, and the occult. This lore had an impact on Rimbaud's poetic vocabulary and encouraged him to daydream about a utopian future.

More practically, Bretagne allowed Rimbaud to use his address in his personal correspondence, thus protecting his mail from his mother's eyes. Bretagne had become friendly with the poet Paul Verlaine—the very

writer whom Rimbaud had singled out as one of the few
worthy living poets of the day. Perhaps Bretagne hinted
to Rimbaud that Verlaine was susceptible to the charms
of young men, for Rimbaud seems to be alluding to his
own availability in his letter to Verlaine, as well as in the
five provocative poems Rimbaud included. In the letter
he promised he'd be no more bother to Verlaine than
"Zanetto" if he came to Paris, referring to an androgynous
young wandering minstrel in a play in which Sarah
Bernhardt had first made her mark two years earlier (as a
young woman playing an ephebe). In one of the poems
Rimbaud included, he pictures five hungry children with
their little rumps in the air looking in a window at night
as a baker plunges his arm into a "black hole" and bakes
bread that makes them sigh with longing. It's a piece of
soft-core kiddie porn posing as Hugo-style social bathos.
In another poem, a group of French smugglers who
transport contraband across the border are stopped and
felt up by German border guards. In yet another, a priest
is squatting and struggling to shit. In his letter Rimbaud
detailed his artistic likes and dislikes and said that he was
bored to the point of extinction in Charleville. He wrote
Verlaine that his mother gave him only ten centimes a
week—to put directly into the collection plate at church.

Without waiting for a response, Rimbaud sent off a few
more poems to Verlaine two days later. Then came the
fateful response from Paris: "Come, dear great soul, we
call you, we await you." Verlaine enclosed the train fare.

Verlaine, as it turned out, was a homicidal alcoholic. He was also an extremely gentle, sensitive poet with a distinctive tone and a remarkable musicality. These two aspects of his character had set up a pitched battle over his anguished destiny; he would always be susceptible to one impulse or the other.

Like Rimbaud's, Paul Verlaine's family had its origins in the Ardennes. Like Rimbaud, Verlaine had a military man as a father, though throughout most of Verlaine's adolescence and early adulthood his father was an "invalid": he had cataracts and he had lost a lot of money in investments. Today these problems might be resolved with dispatch by a surgeon, a shrink, and a financial adviser, but at the time they constituted a good reason for remaining close to the fire and seldom venturing out into the world. In short, they signaled the end of an active life.

There was something decidedly morbid about the Verlaine family. Verlaine's mother had had two full-term miscarriages and preserved the fetuses in a pair of large clear bottles of alcohol in the family home. At last she gave birth to a living baby, little Paul, on March 30, 1844, making him ten years older than Rimbaud.

Like Rimbaud, Verlaine had been a brilliant student in classical languages and had written dazzling verses in Latin. But there the resemblance ended. Verlaine was a lazy, always dirty boy who barely squeaked by in most of his classes. And unlike Rimbaud's, Verlaine's mother was a silly, indulgent woman who endlessly forgave her son's failings and excesses. Whereas Rimbaud's looks were striking, if strange, Verlaine was indisputably ugly, resembling the popular idea of Socrates while possessing none of the philosopher's equanimity. His skull was too large, his face pushed in, his eyes oblique, his pug nose too small and tipped up. He'd lost most of his hair at an early age and compensated for it by growing sparse, wispy whiskers. The mother of Verlaine's best friend said after meeting him, "My God, your friend made me think of an orangutan escaped from the zoo!" And years later, when Verlaine became notorious for his violence and alcoholism, one of his old teachers would say, "I never doubted that there was something in that hideous head which resembled a half-witted criminal."

Whereas Rimbaud seems to have shown no erotic interest in his own sex before meeting Verlaine, the older poet was notorious at school for groping his classmates. He fell in love with one, Lucien Viotti, with whom he stayed in close contact for more than a decade. At one point he even began to collaborate with Lucien on the libretto for an operetta. When Lucien joined the army in 1870, received a gunshot in the foot, and was placed in a German hospital where he contracted the chicken pox and died, the bereft Verlaine could only blame himself for having earlier broken off with the young man in a moment of homosexual panic. He wrote a passionate page about Lucien in which he lamented the loss of "your elegant and refined twenty-year-old being, your charming head, the exquisite proportions of your ephebe's body concealed under a gentleman's suit."

After high school, Verlaine enrolled in law school in Paris but seldom attended classes. He spent most of his time reading poetry old and new and getting drunk on absinthe. This drink, long-banned in most countries in the world, was thought to enhance creativity and stoke up the sex drive. Absinthe contains wormwood and has been blamed for bringing on psychotic breaks and inducing hallucinations (Oscar Wilde said that it produced in him the feeling of tulips being trailed along his legs). In Degas's painting *The Absinthe Drinker*, a woman sits in a vacant stupor before her glass. An intense emerald color, the spirits are very strong and bitter and taste like paregoric. In Verlaine's day, drinkers would dilute "the green fairy" with cold water poured through a perforated spoon that held a sugar cube, a ritual that fascinated its adepts in much the same way that the spoon, the flame, the needle, and the tourniquet seemed poetic to heroin addicts in the 1950s.

Verlaine drank so much that he soon succumbed to a special form of crazy and violent alcoholism called *absinthism*. Eventually he withdrew from law school and began working a boondoggle his parents had found for him at the city hall, where he showed up at ten in the morning, took a two-hour sodden lunch, lurched back to the office for an hour or two of shuffling papers, and was ready for aperitifs at the Café de Gaz by five. Notwithstanding his habits, Verlaine remained intensely interested in the arts in general and in poetry in particular. He became the art critic for one journal and defended Baudelaire in print, announcing—in the spirit of Art for Art's Sake—that "the goal of poetry is the Beautiful and the Beautiful alone without any reference to the Useful, the True or the Just." By the mid-1860s Verlaine was one of the thirty-seven Parnassians in good standing and published from time to time in their poetry journal, *Contemporary Parnassus*. His work was largely ignored by the general public but was ultimately acclaimed over the next few years by fellow poets Stéphane Mallarmé and Victor Hugo, who acknowledged its delicate music and genuine lyric impulse.

Curiously, Verlaine, who would be known in his life as a brutal husband and an impious wretch, as a writer became celebrated as the greatest Catholic poet in the French language (for his collection *Wisdom*), and as an ardent defender of married bliss (*The Good Song*). Verlaine was full of contradictions—by turns wildly exalted and deeply depressed, leading one friend to quip that he was both a clown and an undertaker. One thing is certain: he was beset by strong homosexual desires but hated his "vice" and longed to be rid of it. In Verlaine's mind, this struggle was staged as a contest between bourgeois calm and respectability on the one hand, and on the other hand the lurid but exciting depths of bohemian depravity.

He moved more and more in an artistic milieu. Every week he attended a salon frequented by the composers

Berlioz and Wagner and the painters Édouard Manet and
Henri Fantin-Latour and all the Parnassian band, who
grew accustomed to Verlaine's habits; when he started
drinking absinthe, they made sure to hide the knives.
They knew that in a matter of moments he could go
from the meekest mildness to the most murderous and
ungovernable of rages. One night when he was blind
with drink and wanted money from his mother so that he
could continue his rout into the dawn hours, he became
so angry with her for holding out on him that he attacked
with his cane the jars containing Madame Verlaine's
miscarriages, smashing the glass and dismembering
the tiny rubbery fetuses and scattering them across
the floor—and remarking soddenly that they, like him,
had been macerating in alcohol long enough. The next
morning, Verlaine crawled to his mother's side, begging
her forgiveness in a prolonged, tearful scene of penitence.
As she would do each time for the rest of her days, she
forgave him. On another evening, Verlaine threatened
his mother with a saber, attempting to extort 200 francs
from her. Luckily, his aunt and his companion of the
evening were able to restrain him. Verlaine also attacked
a close friend, the novelist Edmond Lepelletier, as well as
the fashionable right-wing writer Alphonse Daudet.

In July 1869, the same month Verlaine nearly killed
his mother, he published his second book, *Fêtes Galantes*,
a collection of poems dedicated to the early eighteenth-
century painter of courtly seduction and aristocratic
dalliance, Watteau. With his unerring powers of under-
standing the essential, Verlaine (who in truth had only

ever seen one or two Watteaus) managed to divine the bitter melancholy that lay just under these scenes of pastoral pleasure—of lutes and slender barks outfitted with silken sails, of pretty young women in satin gowns beneath translucent parasols, of yearning swains and ancient leafy trees and flower-strewn paths. In his poem "Sentimental Conversation," two lovers, now ghosts, pace through a park and discuss their former passion—he with remembered ardor, she with cool detachment:

> "Do you still remember our ancient ecstasy?"
> "Why would you want me to remember that?"
> "Does your heart still beat faster when I'm mentioned?
>   Do you still see my soul in your dreams?" "No."
> "Oh, the fine days of ineffable happiness when
>   We joined our lips together!" "It's just barely
>   possible."
> "How blue the sky, how great our hope!"
> "Hope has fled, vanquished, toward the black sky."
>   In this way they walked through the wild grasses
>   And the night alone heard their words.

Verlaine was constantly going on the wagon and falling off again. Alarmed for his future, his family insisted that he submit to the discipline and presumed orderliness of marriage.

In the fall of 1869 he met a sixteen-year-old girl, Mathilde Mauté de Fleurville—to give her full (and probably invented) poetic name. She was prettily chubby in the approved fashion of the day, and painfully innocent. She saw Verlaine two or three times at a literary salon and a musical evening before he noticed her. By the time they spoke she was used to his ugliness and greeted him with a friendly smile, and he was charmed by her freshness and kindness. She noticed how gentle and radiant he became around her. She was soon wonderfully moved by the poet's devotion and talent. As she later recalled, "At that moment he ceased to be ugly, and I thought of that pretty fairy tale, Beauty and the Beast, where love transforms the Beast into Prince Charming."

Quite sensibly, Mathilde's father did not want his sixteen-year-old daughter even to consider the suit of a much older man. He urged her to wait two years, but she was smitten. Verlaine had been introduced by Mathilde's own half-brother, a young composer who moved in the same bohemian circles as the poet, had witnessed his drinking, and heard rumors of his homosexuality—though sexual identity did not seem set in stone in the nineteenth century, and artists had a code of honor to forgive one another's "eccentricities." And as Mathilde later wrote, her brother had "lived his whole life full of illusions about everything and everyone."

Although Verlaine was committed to the impersonal elegance of the Parnassians, he immediately set to writing a passionate autobiographical celebration of his courtship of Mathilde, "*La Bonne Chanson*" ("The Good Song"). In short, rhyming lines, Verlaine displayed his characteristic lightness of touch. No wonder that one of his lyrics, "*L'Heure Exquise*" ("The Exquisite Hour"), was later set to music by Proust's dandified young composer-lover Reynaldo Hahn. And no wonder that the impressionable young Mathilde, just "coming out" in society, would fall under the spell of the talented, devoted poet, especially since during the months of their engagement she never once saw him drunk. He attended family dinners at her parents' Montmartre house with sobriety, respect, and great regularity. He made a good impression even on the skeptical Monsieur Mauté. On August 11, 1870, a few weeks before the Prussians laid siege to Paris, Verlaine and Mathilde were married. As she wrote in her memoirs years later, "I can say in all sincerity that when I married Verlaine I loved him as much as he loved me." Verlaine's wedding present was "*La Bonne Chanson*"—which Victor Hugo, making a nod to its publication during the siege of Paris, called "a bouquet in a cannon shell."

The young Verlaines moved into an apartment on the Left Bank looking out on the Île St.-Louis and Notre Dame, near the famous 400-year-old restaurant La Tour d'Argent. As the siege drew out, Verlaine became more and more wild-eyed in his commitment to what he called "the revolution," at least on the level of rhetoric. In practice he was a total coward and did everything to avoid active service. He might have crossed paths with Rimbaud during the adolescent's visits to Paris, but they were not destined to meet till the following fall.

By that time Verlaine was drinking again, could barely tolerate his in-laws and their long, decorous dinners; and his wife, increasingly uneasy about her husband's hours and irritability, had discovered that she was pregnant. Verlaine, who'd continued to work at the Town Hall under the Commune, now found that he'd been fired for his pains by the victorious Versailles government. Verlaine never had a fixed government position again, though for the moment Mathilde's father simply increased the young couple's allowance to compensate for the loss of his salary. To save money Verlaine and Mathilde gave up their apartment and moved in with her parents in their spacious Montmartre apartment, which only set Verlaine's nerves further on edge.

Into this snug, middle-class world Rimbaud entered like an invited catastrophe. He arrived with what would prove to be his greatest poem, the 200-line "The Drunken Boat," a poem to the sea by someone who had never seen it. "The Drunken Boat" had obviously been influenced by Baudelaire's equally long "*Le Voyage*," which also posits dreamscapes of exotic climes and intense, trippy colors. It, too, keeps coming back to the reveries of neglected or abandoned children. It, too, sweeps the reader along in beautiful, unending cadences and subtle but insistent rhymes.

If Baudelaire is one influence, illustrated adventure magazines of the period are another (*Le Magazine pittoresque*, for instance), with their pictures and stories of exploration in the desert, the jungle, and at the Poles, and of floating islands haunted with the roaring of lions and panthers. Rimbaud also read boys' adventure stories by Jules Verne, especially *Twenty Thousand Leagues Under the Sea* with its sunlight split into rainbows in the depths, and James Fenimore Cooper (perhaps the source of the "Redskins" at the beginning of the poem). Edgar Allan Poe also influenced the poem through his descriptions of the Arctic Ocean in *The Narrative of Arthur Gordon Pym*. Critics often claim that creative sparks fly when themes and techniques of genre literature are elevated to the status of high art—and

Rimbaud was one of the first poets of the modern era to understand this principle.

Rimbaud had read widely and unsystematically during his months of idleness in Charleville. "The Drunken Boat" is far-reaching and refers to everything from the *Monitor* (the ironclad Northern warship in the then-recent American Civil War) to the Behemoth, a monster in the Old Testament Book of Job. Moreover, Rimbaud was influenced by "illuminism," a heady mixture of pseudo-science (such as mesmerism and phrenology, or reading character from the shape of the skull), Asian religions, and the belief in the transmigration of souls, exalted theories of electricity and flight and spiritualism and so on. Through Bretagne he had read old books devoted to alchemy, or the secret of eternal life and the magical conversion of base metals into gold.

In addition to these gaudy bits and pieces of knowledge and myth, Rimbaud was able to draw on his own linguistic powers. At least half a dozen words in "The Drunken Boat" are ones he coined, and just as many are obscure words borrowed from his own dialect of the Ardennes.

Equally remarkable is what the poem is not. He has banished from it all of his earlier puerilities. He no longer is parodying other poets nor attacking the church in sacrilegious exaggeration nor defaming women through sexual innuendo. His love of the obscene and the revolting (feces, filth, fleas, diarrhea) has been tempered. All this adolescent tomfoolery has given way to the description of a voyage that is both an actual odyssey and a spiritual saga. The poem begins in the middle of an action (and with a contradiction): "As I was descending the unnavigable Rivers"—the French word is "impassive," which usually means "imperturbable," but here should be linked to the root meaning of "impasse." The boat-towers (*haleurs*) have been killed, used by the Redskins as targets. Now the boat is stripped of its crew and indifferent to its cargo—it is free to travel wherever chance and the currents might take it.

Rimbaud would come back several times in his writing to this theme of "going with the flow"—of floating free from civilization and its strictures. For the first time, these restraints are identified with "Europe's ancient parapets." The boat exchanges these known castles for the flowers of Florida, the freezing waters of the Arctic, for putrid swamps where the rotting carcass of Leviathan (an Old Testament sea monster) lies caught. Glaciers, giant serpents, black seahorses—the drunken boat goes reeling through all these extremes of exotic seascape:

And from then on I was bathed in the Poem
Of the Sea, which was steeped in stars and turning
    milky white,
Absorbing the green blues; in the sea a pensive
    drowned man—
bloated, livid and enraptured—sometimes sank past
    me

But the language does not represent just a travelogue. It also refers to itself specifically as poetry. First of all, those "Rivers" and floating "Peninsulas" are suspiciously capitalized, as if to assure us that they are symbolic or allegorical, not merely places but also Ideas.

The narrator of course is the errant boat. The stanzas are introduced with the words "I was," "I know," "I saw," "I dreamed," "I followed," "I ran against," "I would have wanted," "I drifted," "I saw," and "I no longer can." The highly colored emotional and sensory experiences of the boat constantly remind us of the perception at the heart of the poem; this is no mere concatenation of weird phenomena, but rather sights and sounds occurring to a sentient being. Toward the end, the poem takes a dark turn:

> But it's true I've wept too long! Dawns are
>   heartbreaking,
> Every moon is ghastly and every sun bitter;
> Acrid love has pumped me full of intoxicating
>   drowsiness.
> O may my keel explode! O let me sink at sea!

The poem ends not with a triumphant crossing of the open seas or a shipwreck, but rather with a little boy crouching beside a puddle and sailing a toy boat. This final image is all the homelier and more localized since the word Rimbaud uses for "puddle" is an odd dialect word from the Ardennes—*flache* instead of the usual *flaque*. In short, Rimbaud ends his poem where Baudelaire had begun his—with a child daydreaming of travel:

> Ah! How vast the world is by the light of lamps!
> To the eyes of memory how the world is small!

We learn that the narrator is not the boat, but the child longing to voyage—one already convinced the trip will be tragic.

Rimbaud's poem is a widely acknowledged masterpiece of subtle rhymes, but rhymes so relaxed they are almost undetectable, particularly under the assault of such shocking imagery and complex, sinuous syntax linked through a complexity of present and past participles and phrases placed in apposition to nouns—a grammar that is in fact constantly proposing hypothetical scenes that blend into a palpable reality and then dissolve again into something past, half-recalled. The boldness of this language, syntax, and sequencing is all the more striking because the verse adheres to the classical French measure, the twelve-syllable alexandrine celebrated by the seventeenth-century playwrights Corneille and Racine. This was the standard French meter, comparable in English to Shakespeare's blank verse or iambic pentameter. Where Rimbaud introduces an invigorating new variety into this meter is in the caesuras, those pauses within the line—sometimes one, sometimes two, constantly shifting their position from early to late in the long line. (Traditionally the caesura came after the sixth syllable.) Every element of Rimbaud's poem—semantic, rhythmic, linguistic—is calculated to destabilize the reader while placing him or her firmly within a classical grid. Because of the steady underlying regularity, the reader is forced to recognize every poetic extravagance on the surface.

On September 24, 1871, Rimbaud took the train from Charleville to Paris—less than a month before his seventeenth birthday.

All he had with him were his manuscripts ("The Drunken Boat" taking pride of place) and a change of clothes—garments that his mother had sewn for him out of cheap cloth by the bolt and that he'd already outgrown. No one was there to greet him at the train station in Paris. Paul Verlaine, in his confusion and exaltation, kept running back and forth between the Gare du Nord and the nearby Gare de L'Est, accompanied by a young comic poet named Charles Cros. (Cros was also an inventor who very nearly invented the phonograph, though Edison would beat him to it by a month and with a better process.) At last Verlaine and Cros gave up and went back to Montmartre and Mathilde's parents' house, a fifteen-minute walk away. There in the small cosseted salon they found the young belligerent poet with his sunburned face and large hands, his piercing blue eyes, unsmiling mouth, uttering monosyllables in his heavy Ardennes accent.

Twelve years later Verlaine would recall, "The man was tall, well built, almost athletic, with the perfectly oval face of an angel in exile, with unruly light chestnut hair and eyes of a disquieting blue." Elsewhere Verlaine wrote: "He had a real baby's head, plump and fresh on top of a big bony body with the awkwardness of an adolescent who has grown too quickly. His voice, with its heavy Ardennes accent (almost a patois), broke between bass notes and high squeaks."

The new young genius was displaying the curt manners he must have picked up during his previous visits to Paris. The obedient schoolboy had been replaced by the long-haired, sneering, shabbily dressed brute. Mathilde and her mother snobbishly ascribed the brutishness to countrified naïveté. They were only able to put the boy up for the moment because Monsieur Mauté was away on a hunting party. When Monsieur Mauté returned, however, young Rimbaud would have to be hidden away as someone unsuitable for respectable company. As Mathilde, who was close to his age, much later recalled, "His eyes were blue and rather beautiful, but they had a sly expression which, in our indulgence, we mistook for shyness." She noticed his red peasant's face and his look of a schoolboy who has outgrown his clothes, since his hiked-up trousers "revealed his blue cotton socks knitted with his mother's care." Rimbaud ate much and said little, replying to Charles Cros's questions about his plans and his theories of verse-making with simple grunts. As soon as the gawky adolescent had cleared his plate he lit up his pipe, his "mug-burner" (*brûle-gueule*), smoked it pestiferously, and then shoved off to bed. The super-polite Mautés, mother and daughter, were stupefied by the boy's bad manners, which for the moment they preferred to see as "rough" rather than belligerent. Verlaine retired to read "The Drunken Boat," which he instantly recognized as a turning point in French poetry.

Rimbaud was an impossible guest. He took to nude sunbathing just outside the house. He turned his room into a squalid den. He mutilated an heirloom crucifix. He was proud of the lice infesting his long mane and even pretended he was encouraging the vermin to jump onto passersby. Verlaine was delighted with Rimbaud's antisocial antics, which recalled to him his own younger excesses before his marriage. Verlaine had married partly as a way to straighten out his life and curb his dangerous alcoholism, and yet drinking and carousing were intimately linked to the bohemianism that inspired his poetry. Now he could let his young comrade live out all his rebelliousness for him—while looking sober and sane by contrast.

Verlaine and Rimbaud were both great walkers, and as they strode down the boulevards the older man listened to the younger develop his revolutionary ideas about art, about the need to destroy the old world and to create a new world as the domain of poetry alone. Verlaine had a problem—literally and figuratively—keeping up. Years later he would recall with astonished admiration Rimbaud's powerful legs, the legs of a born walker. Suddenly Verlaine felt that he was being called back to his true destiny, and his enthusiasm increased as he gazed into those ice-blue eyes and listened to that strange Northern burr, which, as the weeks rolled by, was all too quickly rubbed down into a conventional Parisian accent. Verlaine introduced Rimbaud to his friends in the cafés where they congregated regularly. The photographer Etienne Carjat took his picture—the most famous image of the young poet that exists, showing the young genius Rimbaud with his untamed hair, Alaskan-husky blue eyes and uncertain—or perhaps cruel—mouth. Verlaine's poet friends gave frequent dinners, "*Les Diners de Vilains Bonshommes*" ("The Dinners of the Dreadful Goodfellows"), where everyone became rowdy and eloquent—and where Rimbaud circulated a copy of the improbably rich, startling verses of "The Drunken Boat." Rimbaud immediately took to absinthe and sang its praises in a letter home to Delahaye, saying drinking it "was the most delicate and shivery of all habits," although after getting drunk on it you ended up "sleeping in shit."

One of Verlaine's friends, Léon Valade, wrote the next day to an absent member, "You missed a great deal by not being there. A most daring poet not yet eighteen was introduced by Paul Verlaine, his inventor and in fact his John the Baptist. Big hands, big feet, a wholly babyish face like a child of thirteen, deep blue eyes! Such is this boy, whose character is more anti-social than timid and whose imagination combines great powers with unheard-of corruption and who has fascinated and terrified all our friends." The modern reader can't help but smile at the readiness of Parisians of that epoch to be "terrified" by "unheard-of corruption." In fact these very poets would soon form the core group of the Decadents (a "school" that took its name from a line by Verlaine: "I am the

Empire at the end of its decadence"). Valade concluded by calling Rimbaud "Satan in the midst of the doctors," as opposed to Christ among the rabbis at the Temple. When one of the Goncourt brothers (the most famous diarists of the era) shook Rimbaud's hand, he claimed that he felt as if he were touching the most notorious murderer of the day.

And yet some of the Parisians thought Rimbaud was downright ugly. Even his childhood friend Ernest Delahaye would assert, "His only beauty was in his eyes, a pale blue through which a dark blue blazed!—the most beautiful eyes I've seen—with an expression of bravura ready to cut through everything when he was serious and, when he laughed, of a child's exquisite sweetness—and his eyes were almost always astonishingly deep and tender."

Indeed, Verlaine himself later recalled that right off the bat few of the Parnassians liked Rimbaud. In fact, most of them disliked or detested "the new phenomenon."

Perhaps Rimbaud's most outrageous remark was his suggestion to the great Parnassian guru Théodore de Banville that the alexandrine (the traditional French meter) should be done away with entirely. For Banville, who believed in traditional forms, this was heresy—or a hilarious bit of cheek. What he didn't realize was that Rimbaud was about to invent the prose poem. To be sure, Baudelaire had already experimented with prose poems, but Rimbaud would subtract the casual, descriptive, anecdotal aspect of those pieces and replace it with an orphic kind of utterance that was more visionary and more difficult, not less, than the verse of the day. For Rimbaud the prose poem would be cold and sublime. It would also undeniably be poetry—lyric and compressed, highly visual, and intricately patterned. And for Rimbaud the prose poem would strain meaning to the very limits—farther into the obscure than it had ever ventured before.

Monsieur Mauté, Verlaine's father-in-law, was due to return, and Charles Cros took Rimbaud in briefly—until he used as toilet paper a magazine in which Cros had just published some of his poems. Next Banville offered to take in the young poet and lodge him in the maid's room above his apartment at 10, rue de Buci—just a few steps from the heart of Left Bank Paris, St. Germain-de-Prés. But even though Rimbaud had only recently written Banville ambiguous letters of admiration from Charleville, now that he was actually in the presence of the smooth, urbane man of letters, he couldn't help but rebel. His first night in Banville's maid's room, he stood in the illuminated window stark naked and threw down his lice-laden clothes into the street.

Within a week Banville had asked the miscreant to leave, but only after Rimbaud had smashed the china in his room, soiled the bed sheets with his muddy boots, and sold some of the furniture. Within a few short weeks after his arrival he was no longer being described as an angel or a devil but as an obnoxious boor. Verlaine's brother-in-law, Charles de Sivry, by all accounts one of the most good-hearted and unsuspecting of men, at last met the genius and was disillusioned to discover "a vile, vicious, disgusting, smutty little schoolboy."

The only person who couldn't see his faults—or who delighted in them—was Verlaine. In the fourteen months since he'd married, Verlaine had written no new poetry, though he had successfully curbed the excesses of his drinking. Now Rimbaud was encouraging him to live like a savage and stay drunk—and to write like the seer he was destined to be. Moreover, Rimbaud represented Verlaine's sexual ideal, a dominant adolescent who appeared to be always available erotically. Thirty years later, Edmond Lepelletier remembered that Verlaine was completely under the spell of his paramour: "Arthur Rimbaud was a tall, gawky young man, very thin, with the look of a rather fierce street Arab. He was taciturn, with a sneering solemnity, very impressed by his own importance, affecting a universal scorn of men and things. He struck Baudelairean attitudes....He conscientiously played the part of sublime child and infant prodigy. Verlaine imposed him on all his circle....Although Verlaine was more than ten years older than Rimbaud, he allowed his despotic companion to lead him about like a child. Verlaine was weak in everything, except poetic talent...."

There are several curious things to notice about this reminiscence. If Rimbaud was self-important and scornful, then this was only coherent with his program to turn himself into a seer. He obviously conceived of the existence of a poet as a role as much as it was a function. In our day, when performance art is ubiquitous and the artist's persona is as finely crafted as the work, Rimbaud's project seems less surprising. Undoubtedly Rimbaud's persona was compounded out of an ambition to fall into becoming neither a colorfully eccentric bohemian nor a stiff-collared Parnassian bourgeois; the only other alternative was to be a monster, to be "impossible." Lepelletier assumes the reader will concur that striking a pose is deplorable, especially a Baudelairean pose, but for Rimbaud, who saw poetry as alchemical, a way of changing reality, poetry could never be merely vocational. It had to involve the whole life and its choices had to begin with a rejection of the conventional.

Not incidentally, if Lepelletier spoke so disobligingly of Rimbaud in 1900, it was partly because they'd had their run-ins in 1871. After Verlaine and Rimbaud strode about the Odéon Theatre lobby arm in arm, embracing each other during an intermission, Lepelletier had written in his gossip column the next day, "Paul Verlaine was arm-in-arm with a charming young lady, Mlle Rimbaut." A few days later, over dinner, Rimbaud threatened Lepelletier with a steak knife, and the older man, according to his own later account, threw the boy back into his seat, "saying as I did so that I had recently been at war and that since I had not been afraid of the Prussians I wasn't going to be intimidated by a little troublemaker like him."

Rimbaud was moved to the headquarters of one of Verlaine's literary groups, the Zutistes. "Zut!" is now a grandmotherly substitute for "Damn!" but at the time it still carried a heavy charge of profanity, a bit like "bloody" then and now. The club, which overlapped with the Vilains Bonshommes, met at the Hôtel des Étrangers on the corner of the boulevard St. Michel and the rue Racine, a block from the Odéon Theatre. The club kept a group album to which all the members, including Rimbaud, contributed ribald sonnets, funny drawings, and parodies of artistic rivals or enemy poets—or of one another. In one example, Rimbaud was especially amused to parody Verlaine's earlier poems, the *Fêtes Galantes.*

By now, Verlaine had given up his respectable clothes and returned to his slouch hat and dirty muffler, and although he and Rimbaud lived like beggars and Rimbaud was constantly being moved from one guest room to another, together the two did manage to spend considerable sums of money—the equivalent, in fact, of an entire year's salary for an office worker. Most likely they lavished it on drink—for themselves and everyone around them. In any case, Verlaine's young wife, Mathilde, became worried, though she dared not confide her anxiety to her parents. She was about to give birth to their child. Once more, Verlaine had turned violent, throwing her to the floor one night in a drunken rage. On another occasion, he threatened to blow up his in-laws' house by igniting the cabinet that contained Monsieur Mauté's hunting cartridges.

Rimbaud was so belligerent that the two lovers found their circle shrinking—especially since they made no secret of their "vice." They collaborated on a sonnet celebrating the asshole ("*Sonnet du trou du cul*")—Verlaine wrote the first eight lines and Rimbaud the last six:

Dark and puckered like a violet carnation
It breathes, humbly lurking amidst the moss,

Still moist from an amorous inclination which
    follows the gentle dip
Of the white buttocks down to the edge of its scarlet
    hem.

Filaments like milk tears have wept
Under the cruel South Wind that pushes them out
Through the little clots of reddened marl
In order to irrigate its beckoning slope.

My mouth often hooks up with its suction cup;
Jealous of literal intercourse, my soul
Turns it into a swamp of tears and a nest of
    sputtering sobs.

It's the shriveled olive and the flute-hugger;
It's the tube that extrudes the heavenly candy;
A Feminine land of Canaan hatched in puddles.

In the album of the Zutistes, Verlaine wrote a "comic"
poem about killing his father-in-law, "the disgusting old
man" (*birbe infect*). In an early essay, Napoleon III had
called for the "end to pauperism." Now Verlaine, in a play
on words, demanded the "end of father-in-lawism" (*beau-
père* meaning "father-in-law," *paupérisme* thus became
beau-périsme). Rimbaud and Verlaine had become such
a difficult couple that when Henri Fantin-Latour did a
group portrait of their circle of poets, *Coin de Table*, he
had to replace one poet, Albert Mérat—whom Rimbaud
had recently gravely insulted—with an awkward last-

minute pot of flowers. And although Fantin-Latour did manage to make Rimbaud look suitably ethereal and angelic, he later confessed that he'd had to order the boy to wash his hands before posing. Rimbaud's hands, large and red and covered with chilblains, made their immediate impression on everyone who met him—as if they had a raw, menacing, peasant-like existence of their own.

Perhaps Rimbaud became still more difficult in November, when, according to Delahaye, he tried hashish for the first time. Between hash and absinthe he was well underway in his long, immense, and systematic disordering of all the senses.

After being expelled from several garrets, Rimbaud ended up with a nineteen-year-old sign painter and caricaturist, Jean-Louis Forain, nicknamed "Gavroche" ("the Scamp," which signified a witty, mocking Parisian kid, named after the plucky street urchin in Hugo's *Les Misérables*). Forain, an ex-Communard exiled by his father from his family (as was Hugo's character), was as dirty and rebellious as Rimbaud; they got along perfectly. He did a drawing of a brooding, baby-faced Rimbaud and captioned it, "If you scratch it, it bites!"

On October 21, 1871, Verlaine's son Georges was born. The birth seemed only to enrage Verlaine all the more. Mathilde later claimed that Verlaine threatened her life every day between October 1871 and January 1872. Just after the new year he attempted to set fire to her hair, but the match went out. "As for the child," she wrote, "Verlaine was absolutely indifferent to him. He never kissed him or looked at him; he simply ignored him." One day in January, after Mathilde refused to give Verlaine money for drink, he seized the three-month-old Georges and flung him against the wall. And then he started to choke his wife.

Until now Mathilde had been successfully concealing her husband's brutality from her parents, even though they were all living under the same roof. But now they could see for themselves the marks on their daughter's throat and, in a flood of tears, she confessed all the horrors visited on her since Rimbaud's arrival four months earlier. Perhaps already foreseeing a separation (divorce would not become legal until 1884), Monsieur Mauté asked a doctor to examine the bruises and to sign a document attesting to what she had suffered. Monsieur Mauté also decided that the couple must be separated. He sent Mathilde and the baby off to a hiding place in Périgueux, where his family lived. He also started proceedings for a separation between his daughter and the fiend—probably designed mainly to frighten Verlaine into reforming.

Verlaine decided he needed time to salvage his marriage. He begged Rimbaud to leave town and return to his mother in the Ardennes—not for long, just long enough to set things right. Perhaps Rimbaud went away all the more willingly because at the most recent meeting of the Vilains Bonhommes ("Dreadful Goodfellows") Rimbaud had provoked everyone by loudly adding "Merde!" at the end of every line recited by a young poet. When Carjat, the very photographer who'd taken the most famous portrait of Rimbaud, lifted

Rimbaud up bodily and deposited him outside the room, Rimbaud drew a knife on him and wounded him lightly. He was, of course, banned from all future meetings of the Goodfellows—which further isolated Verlaine, since the group contained all his closest friends. Perhaps that was Rimbaud's goal (the lover's ultimate ambition): to destroy Verlaine's marriage and friendships so that the older man would be entirely dependent on him. Rimbaud saw himself as an archangel descended to earth to liberate Verlaine from his bourgeois temptations as a man and the tendencies toward prettiness in his poetry. It was Rimbaud who made Verlaine reread the technically brilliant poems of Musset and Leconte de Lisle. It was Rimbaud who convinced him to write in ten-syllable lines (instead of the flowing, automatically eloquent twelve syllables of French tradition or the eight syllables of ballads). And it was Rimbaud who tried to banish human anecdotes, realistic sketches, and sentimental portraits from Verlaine's work. Whereas Verlaine's poetry was all about the past (personal or historical), Rimbaud was one of the rare poets of any epoch who was turned toward the future, and a fairly abstract one at that. Verlaine would announce in letters that he was going to write poems "from which man will be entirely banished." From now on, he said, he would write about "landscapes, things, the aura of things." Which sounds like a good description of Rimbaud's next major work, *Illuminations*, but not of any of Verlaine's poetry.

Something of the tenor of their relationship can be deduced from "Vagabonds," one of the prose poems included in *Illuminations*. In it, Verlaine, "the pitiful brother" (but a paragraph later "the satanic doctor"), complains that Rimbaud's peculiar blend of bad luck and innocence has isolated them and led them into poverty and exile. The "poor brother," with his mouth rotten and his eyes starting out of his head, wakes up every night shouting reproaches—his "dream of idiotic grief"—which prompts the offended, misunderstood Rimbaud to think:

> Actually in all innocence I had undertaken to return him to his original state of Child of the Sun,—and we kept wandering, nourished only by spring water and dry biscuit, as I urgently tried to find the place and the formula.

What was this place and formula Rimbaud was so eager to discover? It undoubtedly had to do with a utopian future that would exclude the deadening effects of conventionality and would usher in a whole new era of love. Again and again he refers to "the new harmony," "the new love," and "the new men." He calls for a "departure" toward "the new affection." And he states at the end of his hashish poem: "We know how to give all our life all the time." Historically, we have entered a period, Rimbaud tells us, that is one of both murderous and pitiless assassins—and of hashish-smokers (*le temps des Assassins*). The original "assassins," we recall, were a fierce Muslim band of hashish-smokers and bandits who flourished from the eighth to the fourteenth century.

Rimbaud could certainly be as pitiless as a real assassin. He once had Verlaine play a "game" in which Verlaine would stretch out his hand on the table and Rimbaud would stab at his spread fingers. Verlaine thought the point of the game was to show that he wouldn't flinch, that he trusted Rimbaud. But Rimbaud quite simply stabbed him in the wrist.

By the beginning of March 1872, just six months after his arrival in Paris—and Verlaine's life—Rimbaud was headed back home to his mother. He knew that he would be back with the older man as soon as Verlaine had straightened out his marriage. Rimbaud also knew that his strategic retreat was only temporary. Eventually Mathilde returned to Paris with their son Georges and for a while everything seemed back on an even keel. Verlaine was even looking for a job again.

Rimbaud remained with his mother for only two months. He sobered up, wrote more poetry, and went to the library, where he studied some pretty eighteenth-century verses, copying them out and passing them along to Verlaine. He sat in the café with his big homosexual friend Bretagne and smoked his pipe—and wrote almost daily to Verlaine, although little remains of their correspondence (ultimately Mathilde would destroy an entire packet of Rimbaud's letters to Verlaine, discovering them after her husband had left her definitively). In one long, newsy letter from Verlaine to Rimbaud, the reader gets a sense of the two poets' relationship, as well as their calculated duplicity toward Mathilde and Verlaine's own mother. Rimbaud has been instructed to send his *lettres martyriques* ("martyred letters," in which he presumably complains of their separation) care of Madame Verlaine. In those letters, Rimbaud was not to mention any possibility of their getting back together. However, in some of his other letters—those sent care of Rimbaud's former roommate Forain—"Rimbe" (as Verlaine calls him) is encouraged to send Verlaine instructions informing him about the life they will soon be living together, "its joys, its torments, hypocrisies, cynical bits, everything that's going to be." Then in baby talk Verlaine adds "Me all yours, all you" (*"Moi tout tien, tout toi"*). Verlaine was given to baby-talk and liked to refer to Rimbaud as "the little fair-haired pussycat."

One of the weirdest features of these letters is the bad English. Both Rimbaud and Verlaine fancied they knew English, but it is of a startling sort. For instance, when Verlaine wants to say he dreamed twice the previous night of Rimbaud as all golden, he writes, *"Toi tout goldez,"* adding in a footnote that goldez means *doré* in English, then commenting modestly, "I forgot you know this language as imperfectly as I do." (*Doré*, incidentally, was underworld argot for a sodomized boy.)

In the same letter Verlaine warns Rimbaud that when he returns to Paris he must put up some semblance of respectability with regard to laundering his shirts, blacking his boots, combing his hair, and producing friendly facial expressions. They both have a creepy, coded way of wishing *"merde"* to each other: *"T'écrire tout celui de ma merde,"* Verlaine writes, and Rimbaud writes eight times, *"Merde pour moi!"*

The poems Rimbaud was writing at the time mark a complete break with his earlier work, as if his practice were catching up with the theory he'd been preaching to Verlaine. Suddenly he has banished the sentimentality and the human interest of his earlier Hugo-like poems. He is keeping the visionary and the orphic aspects of "The Drunken Boat" but expressing them in short lines—often of eight syllables ending in "slant rhymes" in which the vowels alone "rhyme" or, more usually, just the consonants (*"tilleuls / spirituelles,"* *"Nature / je meure"*). Despite their obscurity and impersonality, some of Rimbaud's confusion and grief break through:

> I want the seasons to consume me.
> To you, Nature, I turn myself over;
> And my hunger and all my thirst.
> And if it please you, nourish, water me.
> I have none, not one illusion;
> To laugh at relatives, at the sun—
> But I don't want to laugh at anything;
> Let my bad luck remain free.

In another poem, "The Song of the Highest Tower, "Rimbaud laments wasting his "idle youth" by being subjugated to others (like many egotists, he imagines he's self-sacrificing). "Through politeness / I've lost my life. / Let the era begin / When hearts turn to love." Again and again Rimbaud imagines a future epoch ruled by love; perhaps he was so attracted to universal utopian love in the future because he was so incapable of simple affection in the present for even one other person. In yet another poem of this time, "Eternity," Rimbaud renounces hope and calls for "patience and science," while admitting that he knows "torture" awaits him.

These are the gnomic, intensely private poems of a young man licking his wounds, feeling rejected, abandoning hope, longing for his lover. In a slightly later poem, "O Seasons, O Castles," Rimbaud seems clearly to be envisioning a surrender to Verlaine, the man who will take charge "of my life"—unless the whole poem is to be read as a monologue placed in the mind and mouth of Verlaine. Rimbaud would soon enough be inventing such speeches for his older lover, "the Foolish Virgin," in his extended prose poem, *A Season in Hell.*

Sometime during May Rimbaud returned quietly to Paris, moving from one room to another over the next forty days. He lived at first in a maid's room on rue Monsieur-le-Prince across from the Saint-Louis high school, then at the Hotel Cluny on the rue Victor-Cousin, a room overlooking a quiet courtyard. Verlaine was ecstatic and immediately abandoned all his plans for Rimbaud to find a job—an idea that had prompted Rimbaud to reply splenetically, "Only when you see me literally eating shit, only then will you decide that I'm no longer too expensive to feed." Now that Rimbaud was back in his arms, Verlaine wrote (for Rimbaud's eyes alone) a poem in which he addressed the boy as he might a jealous god—and in which he compared himself to a dying swan. Verlaine was melodramatic about his own excited, erotic abjection, and about Rimbaud's youth and virility—and the cruelty in Rimbaud he kept encouraging.

Rimbaud was working all night every night in his garret and then at dawn going down to a local bar, getting drunk on absinthe and finally staggering back up to his room for a sodden sleep. In literary Paris he was now a pariah, which suited him fine since he had no desire to waste his time talking poetry in cafés. The summer was intermittently very hot, especially up under the eaves. Rimbaud found himself drinking enormous quantities of water and for once longing for the caves and caverns of the Ardennes. As he put it in a letter to Delahaye, who was predictably complaining about life in the provinces, Paris (or "Pamerde" as he called it in a variation on the word for shit) in the warm weather was no better. With typical misanthropy he wrote, "The heat isn't too constant, but to see that the fine weather is to everyone's advantage, and that everyone is a pig, well, I hate summer, which knocks me out when it begins to settle in a bit." He describes the "Academy of Absinthe" at 176 rue St.-Jacques, so called because it had forty casks of absinthe along the walls, just as the Académie Française had forty "immortals" as members. With characteristic spite he wishes that the Prussians would occupy the Ardennes even more thoroughly and ruthlessly, though he seems to miss the Café de l'Univers and his friends, including a new teacher at the Charleville high school, Henri Perrin, a writer and a radical antimonarchist.

Verlaine had promised his wife that Rimbaud would never come back to Paris; that had been the condition of her return with the baby. But now Mathilde could tell from Verlaine's drunken abuse that the boy must be back; someone she knew had even sighted him. Then, on July 7, she sent her husband out to find something she could take for a headache. He never returned. He'd run into Rimbaud in the street, who announced he was leaving for Belgium, that he was fed up with Paris.

As Verlaine later recorded, he said:

"But my wife is ill. I have to go to get something at the pharmacist's...."

"No, you don't. Stop going on about your wife. Come on, I told you, we're leaving."

So, naturally, I went with him.

After all, Verlaine had written Rimbaud asking him for instructions about their future life together; now that Rimbaud had decided, Verlaine could do nothing but obey, and he would never live with his wife again.

Rimbaud and Verlaine must have had a bottle with them since by the time they got off at Arras to change trains, they were acting even more sophomorically than usual. In the station café, when they realized that the man at the next table was eavesdropping, they spontaneously invented conspiratorial dialogue for themselves about their crimes past and future. The man tiptoed away and reported them to the police.

For Rimbaud and Verlaine, the farce that ensued was great fun. Before long the bewildered police chief of Arras had ordered them to board a train for Paris and to return there immediately. Once they were back where they'd started from they caught a train for Charleville and stayed with Bretagne overnight, drank their way through the next day and after nightfall rode in a friend's cart to the nearby Belgian frontier. They crossed it on foot. All this hocus-pocus was due to Verlaine's fantasy that he might be stopped at the border as a former Communard.

Verlaine wrote an oddly affectionate note to Mathilde from Brussels: "My poor Mathilde, Don't worry. And don't be sad. I'm having a bad dream. I'll come back one day." A few days later he sent a second letter in which he claimed he had come to Brussels to do research on the former Communards who'd taken refuge there. Since he was planning to stay for a while to prepare his book, would she mind sending him his papers?

It was then that Mathilde discovered Rimbaud's letters to Verlaine, from which she learned that the two men had been plotting all along to get back together, and that Rimbaud's two-month stay with his mother had always been staged as a farce, a temporary ruse. The letters were obscene and sexual, and in one of these Rimbaud referred to Verlaine's strategy to save his marriage as nothing more than a "whim." Mathilde destroyed the letters as well as a long poem by Rimbaud, "The Spiritual Hunt" (*"La Chasse Spirituelle"*), which Verlaine later claimed was Rimbaud's masterpiece. In his overevaluation of this lost text, Verlaine seems clearly to have been what we might now call a drama queen; he couldn't remember a single line from it later, or even its title.

The two months that Rimbaud and Verlaine spent in Brussels were fairly desperate. They were on permanent holiday, poorly sustained by handouts from Verlaine's mother, their companions the paranoid and stranded French anarchists and revolutionaries whom Rimbaud actually scorned, their sole occupation getting drunk and sleeping it off. They were pursuing Rimbaud's program of "the disordering of all the senses." Strangely, once he started to write during this period of abjection and passion, Verlaine did produce his best collection, "*Romances Sans Paroles*" ("Songs Without Words"), after a musical title by Mendelssohn—a title that paradoxically denies the very function and substance of poetry. Mendelssohn's pieces for solo piano have suggestive titles such as "Contemplation," "Agitation," "Regrets," and "The Brook," and it was a form the composer returned to again and again. And perhaps Verlaine's own title suggested the qualities of vagueness and musicality without eloquence that Verlaine most esteemed in poetry.

Rimbaud had not only been exposing Verlaine to the witty, crisp operetta lyrics of the eighteenth century by Charles-Simon Favart (one of the leading figures of the Opéra Comique), but he'd also been drawing Verlaine's attention to folk songs, the oldest ballads, the simplest forms found in popular verse. Verlaine began turning out some of the purest, most heartfelt lyrical poems in the language. In his "Forgotten Arias," the first part of *Songs Without Words*, Verlaine seems to be debating his competing loves for Rimbaud and Mathilde, though in such short, fragmentary lines that the subject is seldom clear—as if he'd reduced thousands of rose petals to a few drops of what perfumers call "Rose Absolute." And then Rimbaud's own new poems had a direct influence. When Rimbaud writes:

It's been found.
What? Eternity.

(*Elle est retrouvée
Quoi? –L'Eternité*)

his lines are obviously the model for Verlaine's:

In the unbroken
Dullness of the plain
The hesitant snow
Glows like sand

(*Dans l'interminable
Ennui de la plaine
La neige incertaine
Luit comme du sable*)

In another of his poems Verlaine announces that his soul is sad "because of a woman." He specifies:

I am not consoled
Though it was my heart that went away.

In yet another he addresses Rimbaud as if they were both young girls who needed to pardon themselves and wander off far from men and women, "coolly forgetting what has sent us into exile." Verlaine was never one for squarely confronting his problems; at the risk of sounding priggish, one could say that all his glancing ways of staging the tensions of his life make for great verse, if fairly sketchy morality.

Perhaps the civil tone of Verlaine's notes to Mathilde (and her own memories of the good times they'd had as a couple) impelled her to make one last effort to save her marriage. She wrote Verlaine saying that she was coming to Brussels with her mother. She granted him an appointment at the hotel where he'd been staying. By the time she arrived in Belgium he and Rimbaud had checked out, but Verlaine did show up at the designated hotel punctually. He seemed indifferent to Mathilde's talk of a reconciliation until she proposed that they leave their baby with her mother and sail off together for New Caledonia in the Pacific, 700 miles east of Australia—an exotic enough destination to suggest a total renewal of the terms of their union and to fire his imagination.

Verlaine agreed to meet Mathilde and her mother at the train station the next afternoon and return with them to Paris. He showed up, to be sure, but drunk and surly, and when they stopped at the border for the formalities, Verlaine slipped away in the confusion and returned to Brussels and Rimbaud. He wrote Mathilde—probably under the supervision of Rimbaud—a nasty little note:

Miserable carrot fairy, princess mouse, bedbug just waiting for two fingers and a pot, you made me do everything, perhaps you have broken my friend's heart; I am rejoining Rimbaud if he still wants me after the betrayal you forced on me.

Mathilde finally got the message; she handed the letter over to her father, said she wanted a separation—divorce being not possible in France for another decade—and stipulated that she never wanted to hear Verlaine's name mentioned again. When her husband sent her letters, as he did often over the years, she put them unread into a box. Nor did she want Verlaine to have visiting rights with their son. The son, who grew up to be a ne'er-do-well, failed to attend even his father's funeral years later.

Verlaine and Rimbaud went wandering through the villages and countryside near Brussels. They were obviously happy at this renewed commitment. Verlaine wrote poems about the coming of autumn, about an old-fashioned merry-go-round, about a château where they might make love—and about his wife.

With just a little effort, the self-pitying Verlaine had worked things around so that he was the one who'd been abandoned by a wife who was impatient, cold, lacking in sweetness, and indifferent—all faults that could be ascribed to her youth. The poet recalls her light body, her mad kisses—moments that will remain among the speaker's happiest and saddest. Quite literally in this poem (given an English name by Verlaine, "Birds in the Night"), he ends up a martyr—an early Christian martyr who laughs with Jesus as his witness and without moving "a hair of his body, a nerve of his face!"

Rimbaud, in a more somber vein, was writing an ode to Brussels:

Boulevard without motion or commerce,
Dumb, everything a drama and everything a comedy,
A junction of melting scenes—
I know you and admire you in silence.

On September 8, a Sunday, the couple left Ostend for England, sailing to Dover. There they experienced the famous typically shut-down, empty-street English Sunday and had to go to considerable lengths just to buy breakfast. After two days they took the train to London, where they were to live for the next several months, till December.

They were immediately plunged into the life of Soho, which was so full of French exiles and expatriates that they scarcely had any occasion to practice their English. They associated with many of the former Communards, though Verlaine soon gave up his never-very-definite idea of writing a history of the radical movement. And though he would often take on big prose projects—*My Hospitals, My Prisons, Memoirs of a Widower*—that sounded as if they'd be comprehensive and juicily self-revealing, in fact Verlaine usually ran out of steam rather quickly, playing with words and remaining disappointingly discreet. Coming to a market that was already glutted, he and Rimbaud couldn't find work teaching conversational French, but they did both manage to make a meager living doing business translations.

The exact chronology of Rimbaud's works still seems imprecise, but if he wasn't actually working on some of the prose poems in *Illuminations*, then he was storing up strong visual impressions of the crowded, dirty international city for later use. London in those days was usually submerged in a pea-soup fog for days on end. It had an enormous population (3.2 million) and was geographically spread out—the largest city in the world. Rimbaud said it was "as black as a crow and as noisy as a duck." The stink of feet in crowded theaters, the screech of street vendors, the cheekiness of beggars and mudlarks fishing for coins in the Thames, the rachitic thinness of so much of the population, the weird contrast of prudish laws and sluttish excess, the nearly universal public drunkenness, the huge parks where arrogant aristocrats paraded past beggars on horseback or in their carriages—all these contrasts and ghastly excesses fascinated the two Frenchman, who walked for miles every day, observing the shape of the future, for they regarded London as both a warning and a promise of things to come. In a caricature of the time, Rimbaud is shown in a brand-new top hat, and in another he's wearing, more characteristically, a slouch hat and has a long clay pipe in his mouth. He was at once ragged and dandified, the very picture of a bohemian of the day.

Through a French friend, they found a shabby little room on Howland Street in the West End, not far from Tottenham Court Road (since demolished and now the site of the Post Office Tower, the tallest structure in London). Constantly followed and observed by

Scotland Yard because of their association with bomb-throwing French terrorists, the two were careful to cause few disturbances and seemed to pass almost unnoticed during their first London stay. The worst thing Rimbaud seemed to do was play the piano too loudly at home and infuriate the neighbors as he caterwauled songs about camels (words by him, no doubt). He submitted to a magazine a poem that would not be published till years later. An English literary friend learned from Rimbaud how to swear in the vilest possible French, and years later this man of letters could astound French visitors with his toe-curling, inventive curses.

Rimbaud also corresponded with his mother and asked her what could be done about the irregular situation between Verlaine and his wife. From the perspective of his newfound London sobriety, Rimbaud sympathized with Verlaine's alienation from his wife, and especially from his son. He knew that Verlaine worried that all the fuss was calculated to force him to pay Mathilde a larger allowance. But more to the point he also worried that if the Mautés persisted in filing for a legal separation, they would drag Rimbaud's name into the affair as Verlaine's homosexual partner. Rimbaud had just written his last poem in normal verse; he was embarking on his two long prose poems. But what if neither effort made him famous? Did he really want to have his name linked with a homosexual scandal that would make finding all future employment impossible? Rimbaud had in fact always been torn between the two poles of wild rebelliousness and dry-eyed realism. Not even their literary friends in Paris,

Brussels, or London approved of their "vice." Just as radicals in Europe and America during the 1960s would reject homosexuals, the Communards and anarchists drew the line short of "inversion" or "pederasty" or "sodomy." If a revolutionary is a nice manly man, he's acceptable. But if he's compromised by perversion, then he is nothing more than a "corrupt" member of the bourgeoisie.

Verlaine wrote Lepelletier: "Rimbaud recently wrote his mother to warn her about all the things that were being said and done against us."

The redoubtable Madame Rimbaud left Charleville for the first time in years and in Paris met with Mathilde and her parents, without success. Perhaps only a dignified and articulate peasant woman such as Vitalie Rimbaud could have made such a visit seem normal and matter-of-fact. The Mautés looked down on her Ardennais accent, her worn-down shoes, unfashionable dress, and large red hands—the hands and piercing blue eyes recalled Arthur all too vividly. As Mathilde wrote later in her memoirs: "Guess which ambassadress they sent here? Oh, surprise! Rimbaud's mother.... The good lady came merely to ask me to renounce my plans to separate because, she said, that would annoy her son. I received her politely but I don't need to say that her efforts met with no success."

Perhaps because Rimbaud and Verlaine could scarcely support themselves in London, the big city intimidated them. They'd walked everywhere and seen all the sights (in a serious and unironic way in which they would never have devoted themselves to seeing Paris), but they could observe on every side the terrible depths of poverty awaiting the penniless foreigner. If Rimbaud and Verlaine in their absinthe-swilling days in Paris had become the most notorious homosexual couple of the day, then suddenly they were leery of that reputation—especially if they were to be dragged into the courts. The only solution was for Rimbaud to return to his mother once again and for Verlaine to make a last-ditch effort to patch up his differences with Mathilde. And so, toward the middle of December, Rimbaud returned to his mother and Charleville.

As Rimbaud's best English-language biographer, Graham Robb, has pointed out, "Like many inveterate travelers, he was attached to his starting point by a powerful piece of elastic. [...] In the nine and a half years between his first escapade (1870) and his final departure from Europe (1880), he lived on the farm at Roche or in the house in Charleville for almost five years, rarely missing Christmas. To those who cherish the image of the blaspheming vagrant who deliberately wrecked his career prospects, this is the unacceptable face of Arthur Rimbaud: an ambitious young writer who repeatedly returned to live with his mother and often induced her to interfere with his life."

Everyone's plans went awry because Verlaine was so lonely in London that as soon as he got a cold he decided he was dying and convoked his mother, who sent Rimbaud (through an intermediary) the price of a train and boat ticket. Madame Verlaine had already spent some 20,000 francs on her son and Rimbaud—the equivalent to nearly four thousand dollars of the period, a fortune in today's money (approximately $70,000).

Rimbaud was not impressed by Verlaine's grief: "He is like a child left in a room without a light, sobbing with fear."

In Rimbaud's presence once again, Verlaine recuperated quickly and soon the two great walkers were tramping through the outlying London towns of Greenwich and Woolwich and through Kew and Kew Gardens. They were living at 34 Howland Street, Fitzroy Square. Rimbaud was driving Verlaine to finish his *Songs Without Words*, a short book in which every poem was superb. Verlaine was determined to dedicate it to Rimbaud—partly as proof of the "innocence" of their relationship and the high artistic and inspirational tenor of their friendship.

The two men devoted hours to studying English— they even tried to translate their own poems into

English without much success. (Their efforts recall those of Mallarmé, who gave English lessons in Paris but whose few verses in that language are awkward and ungrammatical.) They were just as interested in picking up scatological expressions as a legitimate vocabulary. Perhaps it says something about their relationship as well as their linguistic research that Verlaine was able to write Rimbaud this note in English: "I am your old cunt ever open or opened (I don't have my irregular verbs with me)." No matter that "to open" is perfectly regular.

Like many writers of his day (including Marx somewhat earlier), Rimbaud took out a "reader's ticket" at the British Museum. Like the hacks portrayed in George Gissing's 1891 novel about the impoverished scribbling class, *New Grub Street*, Rimbaud spent his days in the public library where the heat and light were free—a bit like cafés back in Paris where one could sit undisturbed for the price of a coffee. Moreover, Rimbaud could immerse himself in the vast book collections of the British Museum—including books by the Communards not available in France. He attempted to look at pornographic books in French by the Marquis de Sade, but wasn't permitted to—those books being banned for all but a few "specialists."

It wasn't that Rimbaud was purposefully stocking his mind with information and sources for his long poems *A Season in Hell* and *Illuminations*, but simply that he was exposing himself to the most varied kinds of literature (children's books, fairy tales, histories, biographies, poems, doggerel) that would provide him with the rhetorical weapons he would need to lend range and dynamism to those works.

During those weeks in London, Rimbaud worked on an anticlerical poem about Jesus and read voraciously. Verlaine completed *Songs Without Words*—and fretted endlessly over his status as a former sympathizer with the Communards. The police were indeed keeping track of his activities—that's how we know that he took a bag to Victoria Station several days in a row to depart for Paris, and then changed his mind. The police imagined that he was trying to throw them off his scent, but in fact he was probably just his usual indecisive self, and a conflict-torn lover.

At last Verlaine and Rimbaud sailed from Dover to Ostend on April 4. Seven days later, Rimbaud joined his family not at Charleville but at the nearby family farm at Roche. A fire had damaged part of the barn and stables, the harvest had been lost, and the tenant farmer had taken off. The long Prussian occupation had taken its toll.

Rimbaud's sister Vitalie kept a journal. She tells us that the village of Roche, which she was seeing for the first time in several years, had just thirteen houses, around 110 inhabitants, no church or school. Their house, which was on the square, had a big bedroom downstairs (where Vitalie and her mother and sister slept) and two little bedrooms rented out to a lodger. Upstairs the tenant had another room and their brother Frédéric also had a room there; the top floor was an immense attic. The countryside, Vitalie wrote, "was flat, rich and fertile." A kilometer away was the village of Saint-Méry, just as tiny as Roche but with a parish church.

The high point of Vitalie's little narrative occurs on Good Friday, when Arthur arrives, completely unexpected.

She describes their shared joy and delight, then ends with the odd remark, "The day was spent in the closeness of our family and in the knowledge of the property that Arthur scarcely knew, so to speak." Like Vitalie, Arthur was seeing the farm for the first time in years.

The family all pitched in doing repairs and farm work, while Rimbaud went up to the attic and wrote *A Season in Hell*. In May he remarked in a letter to his friend Delahaye: "I'm doing some little stories in prose under the general title: *The Pagan Book* or *Negro Book*. It's foolish and innocent.[...]My fate depends on this book, for which I still have half a dozen atrocious stories to invent. How can one invent atrocities here? I won't send you any stories yet, although I already have three of them."

The book was unlike anything he (or anyone else) had written. He had worked on short prose pieces of fiction before, but this work did not have a plot or characters or dialogue or action or even much by way of description. If there are dialogue and narrative, they are half-erased— the mere signposts or perhaps ruins of previous structures. What does pulse through the whole text is something like a confessional urge, though nothing concrete gets revealed.

The text begins with a page of exalted retrospection, which we guess may be the distilled essence of the sections to come. In fact the last line is: "Ah! I've had enough:— But, dear Satan, I beg of you, an eye less inflamed! And while waiting for a few little acts of cowardice in arrears, for you who love in a writer an absence of descriptive or didactic powers, I tear off these hideous leaves from my notebook of a damned man."

The first long section is called "Bad Blood." Throughout the entire work Rimbaud compares himself to various exotic and "primitive" foreigners—here to the ancient Gauls, later to black Africans, Vikings, and Mongols. The idea is that he so rejects namby-pamby European values that he is at once above and below them, too instinctive and too savage. Rimbaud's sardonic humor comes through as well: "From my ancestors the Gauls I inherited the pale blue eyes, the narrow brain, and the awkwardness in combat. I find my clothing as barbarous as theirs. But I don't butter my hair."

What is most characteristic of the whole poem is its resemblance to a half-heard dialogue, a series of muted ripostes and suggested arguments, reproaches, disagreements. While the first paragraph begins by announcing that the ancient Gauls were his ancestors, the second begins:

> If only I had forebears at any given point in the history of France. But no, nothing.
>
> It's obvious to me that I've always belonged to an inferior race. I'm unable to understand revolt. My race has never risen up except to pillage, like wolves gnawing at a beast they haven't killed.

And while that long stanza ends unexpectedly with a paean to science, progress, and mathematics (praise that contains a lot less irony than the modern reader might suspect), the very next one announces that Christ will not help the poet and that he is condemned to an inferior race. This inferior race is apparently the "bad blood" of the section title. The speaker announces that he will travel; prophetically he says, "My day is over; I'm leaving Europe. The sea air will burn my lungs." He will swim and become bronzed by the sun and smoke and drink liqueurs strong as boiling metal. "I will have gold: I will be lazy and brutal."

But no—the very next paragraph, or "prose stanza," begins with, "We're not going." And so on throughout the work, the reader proceeds through statement and contradiction, assertion and denial. What is remarkable is that this particular rhetorical strategy is highly unusual to poetry, though it is found often enough in polemics or other forms of prose argumentation. Poetry more often aspires to a purity of diction, a freedom from devices, an abstinence from conversational turns in favor of a heightened lyricism. If a poet is *polyvocal*—that is, full of many voices—then he is usually trying to be funny (like Byron in the wonderfully chatty *Don Juan*). But Rimbaud is never funny, though he can be sarcastic. As Michael Bakhtin, the Russian literary theorist, writes: "The world of poetry, no matter what contradictions and desperate conflicts the poet might discover in it, is always illuminated by a unique and irrefutable discourse. Contradictions, conflicts, doubts might remain in the subject, adhere to the thoughts, in the emotions—in a word, in the material—but they do not flow through into the language. In poetry the language of doubt must be written in doubt-free language."

A Season in Hell seems written intentionally to contradict this statement. Littered with the fossil-forms of debate, it moves in full dialectical force from conflict to doubt. In his other freestanding long poem, *Illuminations*, Rimbaud did manage to write pure poetry—exalted and univocal. It is the diametrical opposite of *A Season in Hell*. Though these two books were written almost back to back (as can be said of any two works in Rimbaud's oeuvre, since his writing life was so short), they explore two opposing poles of inspiration. *Illuminations* is often glacial, futuristic, and impersonal, whereas *A Season in Hell* is—starting with its title—retrospective, post-Christian, and autobiographical.

In the dialectical motion of *A Season in Hell*, Rimbaud imagines the life of a downtrodden tribesman in Africa living in pain, sin, and ignominy. Then the whites arrive; the speaker is baptized, given clothes and work. He's saved! The speaker becomes nearly hysterical with the prospect of saints and paradise—and then comes crashing down with the lines: "One long farce! My innocence is enough to weep over. Life is a farce led by everyone."

In the concluding stanza of "Bad Blood," the poet begs the firing squad to shoot him down; then he adds bitterly, "I'll get used to it, which is the French thing to do, our idea of honor."

The next section is titled "Night of Hell." The poet toys with the idea that hell might really exist. Perhaps it exists only for Christians ("I believe I am in hell, therefore I am" and "Theology is serious, hell is down below"). He imagines the fire and even the pitchfork. At a certain point it seems he's being punished for his anger and his pride. As an example of his pride, he announces, "I have all the talents," and claims he can make gold out of base metals and even disappear.

In the section called "Delirium I: Foolish Virgin, Infernal Bridegroom," he puts words in the mouth of Verlaine (the foolish virgin) as she suffers over the agonies inflicted by Rimbaud (the bridegroom). The virgin (named after Christ's parable in Matthew about the souls unprepared for the coming of Christ) complains that as she waits for the Lord she is beaten by "this other one." She is at the bottom of the world. She suffers and sobs. His blows truly wound her. She calls for succor from her women friends: "I am a slave to the infernal Bridegroom."

As for the Infernal Bridegroom, "he was almost a child.[...]His mysterious delicacy seduced me. I forgot all my human obligations in order to follow him. What a life! Real life is lacking. We do not belong to the world. I go where he goes, I have to. And often he is carried away against me, against me: the poor soul. The Demon! He's a Devil, you know, he's not a man."

Stylized as this language is in its broad strokes, laid down roughly, one sentence against the next like the burin's gouges in a woodcut, nevertheless we are as close as we will ever be to the actual words these unhappy lovers exchanged and to the real tenor of their stormy relationship.

He says: "I don't love women. Love must be reinvented, that we know. Women can only seek out security. Once they're secure, they lay aside their warmth and beauty; all that remains is cold disdain, the food of modern marriage. Or, on the contrary, I see women marked by happiness, whom I could have made into good comrades, but they're devoured right away by brutes as sensitive as butchers...."

While one of Rimbaud's rants is against marriage, another is his familiar boasting/lamenting that he is from an "inferior" race. As the virgin exclaims:

I have listened to him turning infamy into a form of glory, cruelty into a charm: "I am of a distant race: my ancestors were Scandinavian: They pierced their sides and drank their blood. I shall gash my body all over and get tattoos; I want to become as hideous as a Mongol; you'll see, I'll shout in the streets. I want to become mad with rage. Don't ever show me jewels; they'll make me crawl and twist about on the rug. My riches, I want them completely splashed with blood. Never will I work...."

This is a sort of Orientalist fantasy of the cruel pasha and the white, terrorized slave, the Rape of Sardanapulus in words, all gold and red blood and bearded sadists— except that the despot is in this case beardless, a child. Once again we encounter the familiar objection to work, which Rimbaud made in a letter to Verlaine and which the young poet was doubtless repeating now to his family members, who labored in the fields while he stayed alone in the attic muttering to himself.

Rimbaud's aspirations to become an alchemist and to learn a mage's secrets are here reported by his partner: "Beside his dear sleeping body, how many hours at night I stayed awake wondering why he wished to run away from reality. Never did anyone have such a wish. I recognized (without fearing for him) that he could pose a serious danger to society. Perhaps he possessed secrets for changing life?"

We are hovering directly over the unhappy couple when we overhear Verlaine say, "I understand you," which only makes Rimbaud shrug his shoulders. Rimbaud is constantly threatening to leave his partner and take off one day. Frightened, the virgin makes him promise he'll never go away. He does promise twenty times, a lover's promise as empty as "my saying to him, 'I understand you.'" There is a hint of gay consciousness *avant la lettre*: "Or I will wake up and the laws and morals will have been changed—thanks to his magic power—and the world, while remaining the same otherwise, will leave me to my desires, joys and carefree ways."

The whole section—so intimate, so dramatic, worded in such scorching, unforgettable phrases—ends: "He takes up again his manners of the young mother, the beloved sister. If only he were less willful we'd be saved! But even his sweetness is fatal. I submit to him.—Ah! I'm mad! One day perhaps he'll disappear miraculously, but I must be alerted if he soars up to heaven, I must see the ascension of my boyfriend."

Rimbaud concludes: "What a strange couple."

Moving with the by-now-familiar crablike motion of his thought, from one topic sideways into another, Rimbaud (having referred in the previous section to his magical powers, his "talents") now talks about verbal alchemy, his ability to invent a language accessible to all the senses: "I wrote down silences and nights and I notated the inexpressible. I gave a fixed point to vertigo." These linguistic powers allow the poet to see things around him utterly transformed—a mosque instead of a factory, a drawing room at the bottom of the lake, a drop-down placard from vaudeville attached to the scarecrow in the field beside him—and to imagine that the people around him contain multitudes. A dull monsieur is actually an angel, just as an ordinary family is really a litter of puppies. A few poems are written out as verse to demonstrate these new powers as a seer. Rimbaud then recapitulates his brief career, invoking "The Drunken Boat" and "The Stolen Heart": "I had to travel, distract myself from the spells cast over my brain. At sea—which I loved as if it could wash me clean of my impurities—I saw a consoling Southern Cross rise. I had been damned by the rainbow. Happiness was my fatality, my remorse, my work; my life would always be too vast to be devoted to strength and beauty."

In the next sections, "The Impossible" and "Lightning," Rimbaud appears to be wrestling with all his angels and devils at once. He blames the West and its "swamps" for his discomfort, his "malaise": "Here is my mind wanting to take on all the cruel developments that the spirit has suffered since the end of the Orient." The Orient and the Occident are the thesis and antithesis of his thought. It is as if Rimbaud had already decided to leave the West behind, though he is almost afraid to fall into the kitsch of Orientalist claims to wisdom. His mind is all jumbled. Mention of "the mongrel wisdom of the Koran" gives way to thoughts about the sterile aftermath to Christ's glorious original message. The bad habits of the West (drunkenness, tobacco, ignorance, superstition) are far removed from our "primitive homeland, the wise thought of the Orient." Then another part of his mind, speaking on behalf of the Catholic Church, replies that there is nothing he can learn from the Orient, for what he has in mind is not the Orient, but Eden. Philosophy in turn critiques the priests—and Rimbaud ends up attesting once again his belief in science and progress: "Science can't move quickly enough to suit us."

Should he work or should he be a magnificent layabout? Science might be promising, but it moves too slowly. Death might be attractive—but no, he wants to survive, to live on. Perhaps *A Season in Hell* is so appealing to teenagers because it exists on such an exalted and anguished plane. One idea is proposed, even insisted upon, only to be overthrown by the next statement. The gimlet-eyed seriousness of a precocious adolescent who has already lived hard, who has defied society, who has staked everything on his genius but isn't sure of winning, and who is already bitter—all these twists and turns of bruised thought and offended feeling are captured perfectly in these pages.

In the same conflicted but cautiously optimistic spirit, Rimbaud begins to conclude his text with a short section called "Morning" in which he announces that "today" he has come to the end of relating his tale of Hell. Now he looks up like one of the shepherds for the star and for the three wise men—the heart, the soul, and the mind. He anticipates the day when we can cast aside superstition and become the first worshippers to celebrate "Christmas on earth."

With a typical contradiction, he states that the heavens are singing and the nations are marching. "Though still slaves," he writes, "let us not curse life."

In the very last section, "Adieu," Rimbaud seems to imagine a return to London, which he apostrophizes as "the enormous city with its skies spotted with fire and mud. Ah! The rotting rags, bread soaked in rain, the drunkenness, the thousand loves that have crucified me!" He then acknowledges all that he has invented with his imagination—and bids it farewell: "I created all the festivals, all the triumphs, all the dramas. I tried to invent new flowers, new stars, new flesh and new tongues. I thought I'd taken on supernatural powers. Oh well! I must bury my imagination and my memories. So much for my reputation as an artist and storyteller." Indeed the poet seems dedicated to erasing his memory and living in the present: "You must be absolutely modern." With a cool, disabused independence, he concludes: "A fine advantage is that I can laugh at the old misleading loves and strike with shame these lying couples,—I've seen the hell of women down there;—and it seems to me praiseworthy to possess the truth in just one soul and just one body." This is a poem of farewells—to lies, to the extravagant claims of the imagination, to sensuality, to entangling affairs with other people, to Europe, to art, to vice, to the past, and to memory itself. He even says farewell to language: "No more words. I bury the dead in my belly."

A Season in Hell was written in many drafts and in two different periods—the spring of 1873 and later in August. Although this little book reads like a single outpouring, there are actually many suppressed pages (which still exist in discarded drafts) and astute rearrangements of the text. The "pagan book" quickly evolved into an excruciating dialogue with itself about the attractions and repulsions of civilization. At the heart of the book is a half-erased biographical sketch of his life with Verlaine. There are few facts and little scene-painting, but what rings through the whole section "Bad Blood" is the echo of their voices, the rumors of their quarrels, the murmur of Verlaine's prayers and sighs.

Verlaine contacted Rimbaud on May 18, writing from a town on the Belgian border. Always strongly attracted to Catholicism, he was undergoing a brief period as an adherent to the faith. The two poets met several times, but by May 24 they had decided to return to London. By May 27 they were back in the vast city. Soon they had taken a room in Camden Town at 8 Great College Street (now called Royal College Street); as of this writing in 2008, a historical plaque was being planned to designate the house, one of three in a terrace not far from the new station for the Eurotunnel at St. Pancras. This is the only extant Rimbaud-Verlaine house in the London area.

The two poets, despairing of learning English quickly enough to make their living in that language, offered their services as French professors for those who already knew French and wanted nothing but an extra finesse. In the advertisements Verlaine specified that he was a poet; in fact both poets would be present for the lessons. Despite their magnanimous offer, customers were few. They were still living on handouts from Verlaine's mother. Rimbaud was no longer indulging his urges to disorient himself through drink or to sightsee compulsively. He was attempting to set up a regime of order and hard work—and indeed he was working intermittently on *A Season in Hell*. Verlaine, however, was the same slacker as always—and soon enough the two impoverished men fell into a kind of nasty game. They rolled towels around long knife blades till just the tips were exposed—then they lunged at each other; when they drew blood they went off to the pub. The game doesn't sound as serious today as it was then: before antibiotics, any piercing through the bodily envelope, no matter how minor, was potentially fatal.

Verlaine, as a besotted lover always quick to be wounded, grated on Rimbaud's nerves. They had worn each other out with quarrels and the enforced idleness of poverty. In addition, Verlaine, with his sad-sack Catholicism and his guilt over abandoning his wife and son, seemed morally unevolved to Rimbaud, who hoped to transcend the limits of conventionality.

One day, on July 3, Verlaine came back from the market with a bottle of olive oil and a red herring for their supper. Rimbaud, who was watching him through an open window, sniggered and said, "Have you any idea how ridiculous you look with your bottle of oil in one hand and your fish in the other?" For some reason (the heat? the accumulation of petty humiliations?), Rimbaud's insult was decisive. Verlaine set off without packing his bags. He left no money behind for Rimbaud.

Terrified and bereft, Rimbaud ran down to St. Katherine's dock, where Verlaine was boarding a boat bound for Antwerp. Rimbaud gesticulated wildly for

Verlaine to disembark, but he refused. Rimbaud's ensuing letter is so desperate that it scarcely sounds like the scornful, self-conscious Rimbaud:

London, Friday afternoon

Come back, come back, dear friend, only friend, come back. I swear to you I'll be good. If I was surly with you, it was a joke I persisted in, I regret it more than I can say. Come back, everything will be forgotten. What a misfortune that you believed in this joke. For two whole days I haven't stopped crying. Come back. Be courageous, dear friend. Nothing has been lost. You only have to make the trip back. We'll live together here courageously and patiently. Oh, I beg of you. It's for your own good, besides. Come back, you'll find all your things here. I hope by now you know that there was nothing true that was said during our argument. What a terrible moment! But you, when I made a sign for you to leave the ship, why didn't you come to me? Have we lived two years together to come to this? What are you going to do? If you don't want to come back here, do you want me to join you where you are?

Yes, I'm the one who was wrong.

Tell me you won't forget me?

No, you can't forget me.

You are always with me.

Say something, reply to your friend, shouldn't we still go on living together?

Be courageous. Reply to me quickly.
I can't stay here a long time.
Listen only to your good heart.
Quickly, tell me if I should join you.

> Yours for all my life.
> Rimbaud

Quickly, write back, I can't stay here longer than
Monday evening. I don't have a penny to my name,
I can just barely pay to mail this. I've given your
books and manuscripts to Vermersch.

If I'm not to see you again, I'll join the navy or
the army.

O come back, every hour I start to cry again.
Tell me where I can find you and I'll go there, tell
me, telegraph me—I have to leave Monday night,
where are you going, what are you going to do?

The young man, lonely and broke and hungry, waited
at Great College Street in the room that is now known
to Rimbaud aficionados as the house of "the knives and
the herring." In the many, many letters we have from
Rimbaud's hand, this is the one in which he expresses
himself the most nakedly and urgently.

Verlaine wrote him from the ship that he had had to
take off, that this life of violence and scenes could not
go on. He apologizes for being stingy with Rimbaud but
mentions that he intends to buy a revolver, which doesn't
come cheap, nor will three days in a hotel. Then he adds

that if his wife does not take him back within three days he'll blow his brains out. "My last thought, my friend, shall be for you."

Although Rimbaud promised to give up his quarrelsomeness, this letter at once soothed and irritated him. He wrote:

> First of all there's nothing positive in your letter. Your wife will not come or will come in three months or three years, who knows? As for croaking, I know you…
>
> So you're going (while waiting for your wife) to fling yourself about, wander around, bore people. You still haven't realized—you of all people!—that the tantrums were equally ridiculous on each side.

Resorting to shockingly transparent emotional blackmail, Rimbaud adds, "If you do not want to come back to me or if you don't want me to come to you, you're committing a crime, and you'll regret it for MANY A LONG YEAR by losing all your freedom and suffering more atrocious problems perhaps than any you have known till now."

Rimbaud's parental tone of exasperation and menace is suggestive of their entire relationship. When Rimbaud is not deliberately baiting and tormenting Verlaine, he is remonstrating with him to be reasonable, to be grown-up, to be productive. Verlaine is often the frightened child—when he's not drunk and homicidal. He does have a third mood—that of timorous but exalted creativity—

and that is the state of mind that fascinates and excites Rimbaud.

Verlaine in the meantime had decided not to kill himself but to join the Spanish army. Back in Paris, Mathilde wasn't even opening the letters from him, but discarding them in a big drawer. Despite his change of heart, Verlaine, never one to avoid a dramatic opportunity, wrote a fresh suicide note to Madame Rimbaud. The flinty old woman wrote him back a letter full of piety and common sense—a bracing combination:

> At the moment in which I'm writing you, I hope that calm and reflection have come back to your mind. To kill yourself, unhappy man! Killing oneself under such conditions is an act of infamy. Society despises the man who dies in such a fashion, and God himself cannot forgive such a great crime and casts him from his bosom.
>
> Monsieur, I do not know in what manner you have disgraced yourself with Arthur, but I have always foreseen that your relationship would not end happily. Why, you might ask. Because whatever has not been sanctioned and approved of by good and decent parents cannot be good for their children. You young people, you scoff and sneer at everything, but the fact remains that we have experience on our side, and whenever you fail to follow our advice, you will be unhappy. As you can see, I am not trying to flatter you. I never flatter those I hold dear.

What is remarkable is that Rimbaud's mother does not seem concerned with what the neighbors will think. In her austere, morally bizarre vision of the world, all that count are parental authority and God's will. People sometimes label her a prude, but Madame Rimbaud is in fact far too much an uncompromising Jansenist to deserve that label.

Verlaine's moods were extremely labile. He announced in a letter that he was coming back to the love nest of hell in London—and Rimbaud welcomed him, though uncharacteristically, since previously it was he who worried what the neighbors would think. But then, in rapid succession, Verlaine sent a telegram from Belgium:

Volunteer spain come here Hotel liegeois laundry manuscripts if possible

Rimbaud jumped on a train at Victoria Station and by that evening was crossing the English Channel. By the time he arrived in Brussels, Verlaine's mother was present, alarmed by her son's latest suicide threats. Verlaine returned to the hotel soon after Rimbaud's arrival there. He'd been to the Spanish embassy and learned that Spain had no need of foreign volunteers in its army.

By the next evening Verlaine was dangerously drunk. He drank through the night, left the hotel at six in the morning, wandered about till he entered a gun shop at 9:00 a.m. and bought a 7-mm. six-shooter and a box of fifty cartridges. He went into a bar and continued to drink. He loaded the pistol with three cartridges. As the gunsmith later said, "The customer took it away without having mentioned the use to which he was intending to put it."

Had Rimbaud come to Brussels simply because he was broke and it was impossible for him to survive on his own in London? Once he had the Verlaines, mother and son, in his grasp, did he stay around just long enough to squeeze out of them the fare to Paris? Or had he genuinely hoped for a reconciliation with Verlaine? If so, was he put off by Verlaine's drinking and his dwelling on his plans to return to his wife?

As Rimbaud later recalled (about Verlaine):

It is true that at a certain moment he expressed his intention to go to Paris and attempt a reconciliation with his wife. It is also true that he wanted to stop me going there with him, but he kept changing his mind from one moment to the next and could settle on no particular plan.

Perhaps it didn't help that all these discussions were being held in a bar. Rimbaud asked pointedly whom the gun was intended to hurt and Verlaine replied— "jokingly," according to Rimbaud—that it was "for you, for me, everybody." Was he suicidal or homicidal? Did he eventually plan to murder his estranged wife as well?

Rimbaud's English biographer Graham Robb speculates that Rimbaud was planning to blackmail Verlaine and to denounce him as a homosexual—which would most certainly mean that Mathilde would have the grounds for a legal separation and the evidence that Verlaine was not fit to be a father to their son Georges. As Robb puts it:

"For Rimbaud blackmail was the obvious solution. Either Verlaine would be forced to go back and live with Rimbaud, in which case his marriage was certainly over; or, if he complained that Rimbaud had threatened to denounce him as a homosexual, his marriage would be over in any case, since Mathilde would have the evidence she needed."

The question remains: was Verlaine so out of touch with reality that he didn't realize that his wife had already banished him from her life and even from her thoughts and that nothing he could do would ever win her back or even further alienate her? Perhaps Verlaine's blackouts meant that he had no recollection of the horrors he'd already perpetrated on her and his son; or perhaps his bottomless self-pity and paranoia meant that he'd reworked the past in such a way that now he was the victim and she the unreasonable bitch.

When Rimbaud threatened to leave immediately for Paris, Verlaine locked the hotel door and sat down in front of it. After a lively argument, Verlaine pulled out his pistol and shot at Rimbaud. He wounded Rimbaud's wrist and then, in horror at his own actions, dropped the gun, which fired another shot, though the bullet was never found. As Rimbaud testified,

Verlaine immediately expressed the strongest despair over what he'd done; he rushed into the adjoining room occupied by his mother and threw himself on the bed. It was as if he were mad: he put his pistol in my hands and begged me to fire it into his temple. His attitude was one of deep regret for what he'd done.

Verlaine and his mother accompanied Rimbaud immediately to the hospital, where the wound was judged minor and was bandaged. Mother and son begged Rimbaud to stay with them till he was completely cured.

Rimbaud, however, thought the wound was nothing and he wanted to leave immediately for Charleville and his mother's house. Verlaine was once again thrown into despair, but his mother gave Rimbaud twenty francs for his trip and they accompanied him to the train station. Verlaine was very agitated and begged Rimbaud not to leave. He then reached into his pocket where he had put the pistol. Verlaine ran ahead, then turned and came back on Rimbaud, who was convinced he was going to shoot at him once more. Rimbaud took off as fast as he could and accosted a policeman, whom he begged to arrest Verlaine.

Now the fatal legal machinery was set in motion. The constable arrested Verlaine for attempted murder. Before the superintendent Rimbaud made this statement:

For the last year I have been living with Mr. Verlaine. We wrote letters for newspapers and gave French lessons. He had become impossible to live with and I had expressed a desire to return to Paris. Four days ago he left me to come to Brussels and sent a telegram asking me to join him.

Rimbaud mentioned none of the mitigating circumstances—their frequent quarrels, Rimbaud's own contempt for his older friend, the suicide threats, the excessive drinking, or Verlaine's painful relations with his estranged wife. Undoubtedly, Rimbaud was still angry with Verlaine and couldn't calculate the consequences of his statements.

Or maybe Rimbaud was already beginning to feel feverish from the gunshot. He spent the next nine days in a hospital fighting a high fever and having the swollen, infected wound treated in a time before antibiotics. A piece of shrapnel was finally extracted—and exhibited during Verlaine's trial.

Although Verlaine was being tried for attempted murder, the judge and investigators became curious about the immoral relations between the two men. In Rimbaud's belongings they discovered a poem by Verlaine addressed to Rimbaud. It asked:

What hard angel stuffs me full
Between the shoulders, while
I fly off for Paradise? ....

O you, the Jealous one, who waves to me,
Here I am, here is all of me!
Still unworthy I crawl toward you—
Mount my loins and trample me!

Most humiliating, Verlaine was visited by two doctors, who examined his body to "see if he was a homosexual." The doctors remarked on the small penis and its particularly small, tapering head. More significant for them was the anus. They inserted an instrument in it and found that its "contractibility" was almost normal and that there were no injuries. "The conclusion to be drawn from this examination is that P. Verlaine bears on his person traces of habitual pederasty, both active and passive. Neither type of trace is sufficiently marked to give grounds for suspecting inveterate and long-standing habits; rather, they would indicate fairly recent practices." That a contradiction lies at the heart of this diagnosis—a homosexuality at once "habitual" and "recent"—only proves how nonsensical it is.

Ironically, Verlaine had requested just such an examination in the past to prove he was not homosexual; perhaps he thought the whole examination was bogus and could not be made to prove anything. Or maybe his "practices" with Rimbaud did not involve anal intercourse. Here the Belgian doctors seem to have found what they were looking for. They knew that Verlaine was recently divorced and that Mathilde had accused her husband and Rimbaud of immoral relations. The small penis perhaps suggested a low level of virility, its tapering form supposedly spoke of constant insertion in a tight young anus—and the slight dilation of his own anus was thought to prove his submission to Rimbaud's attentions, though all of recent date.

If the reader imagines that such examinations belong to the era of pseudoscience in the nineteenth century, he or she should be reminded that in the English town of Cleveland, from January to June 1987, more than five hundred children were forcibly removed (sometimes during midnight raids) from their parents' homes by social workers because two doctors had determined that they'd all been buggered by their fathers. The doctors were using the highly questionable "anal dilation test," a sort of inserted balloon. If the children couldn't grip the balloon with enough force, the doctors determined that they'd been anally violated. Soon there were no more foster families or hospital rooms in the entire region for the "victims." Ultimately the tide of opinion shifted against the doctors and most of the cases were thrown out of court. The whole unsavory episode was seen as a modern instance of a Salem witch trial. Verlaine's examination by "experts" had no more validity and revealed the same sort of disgusting prurience. As a result of it, curiously enough, we know more about the condition of his penis and anus than we do about the intimate anatomy of any other major poet of the past. The immoral relations between the two poets were confirmed by Madame Verlaine's godson, who lived in Brussels but had never met Rimbaud and scarcely knew Verlaine. The greatest poet of the day, Victor Hugo, wrote Verlaine a note of moral support—if the authorities knew of it, then they seemed unimpressed.

Although Rimbaud, upon reflection, withdrew his complaint against Verlaine, these second thoughts came too late. On August 8, 1873, Verlaine was sentenced to two years in prison and a 200 franc fine—the maximum sentence. Rimbaud had already left the hospital and was spending a few days in a rented room, pale and feverish. A local artist painted his portrait in bed, looking like a little kid with a child's illness—mumps of the soul, perhaps. Before Verlaine's sentence was handed down, Rimbaud took a train (at Madame Verlaine's expense) to a town near the Rimbaud family farm at Roche. He walked the last few miles, locked himself in the dovecote and finished *A Season in Hell* (as he now decided to call it) while sobbing frequently and moaning Verlaine's name. He didn't help his family take in the harvest; he was upstairs harvesting his own bitter fruits. It seems probable that if he had composed earlier in the spring the "Bad Blood" section, then he now wrote out the "Delirium" section and the monologue of the Foolish Virgin (Verlaine). And he must have edited the whole thing anew, placing the older parts in a brand-new order.

Rimbaud had always urged Verlaine to write in eleven-syllable lines, which gives a strange, stumbling gait to verse that a suave poet (like Verlaine) or a magical one (like Rimbaud) could disguise through sustained thought or syntax. Oddly enough, both Rimbaud and Verlaine in this initial period of separation accepted the eleven-syllable handicap, as if they were remaining true to each other in the very pulse of poetry, far deeper than imagery or subject matter.

In "Tears," an older poem, which Rimbaud revised and included in *A Season in Hell* without its original title, he revels in his powers of transformative imagination. He wanders the Ardennes countryside, drinks the juice of a gourd, imagines that his body has become the sign flapping in front of an inn, that the sunset turns the frozen river water to gold—which he cannot drink. And all these "visions" he presents as evidence that he has learned how "to write silences and the nights." He adds, "I notated the inexpressible. I gave permanence to vertigo."

In prison Verlaine was writing his own eleven-syllable poem, a grandiose picture of hell and heaven called "The Crime of Love" ("*Crimen Amoris*," as the Latin title has it). The first stanza sets the tone:

> In a palace of silk and gold in Ecbatana,
> Beautiful demons (adolescent Satans)
> At the sound of a Muslim music
> Made a litter for the Seven Sins out of their five senses.

Soon Verlaine presents an idealized (or villainized) Rimbaud as he first knew him:

> Now the most beautiful of all the evil angels,
> Sixteen years old under his crown of flowers.
> His arms crossed above his necklaces and dangling fringe,
> He dreams, his eyes full of flames and tears.

Yet in spite of the best efforts of the other satanic teenagers to distract him, he resists their caresses:

> And sorrow places a black butterfly
> On his dear forehead afire with gold ornaments—
> Oh, immortal and terrifying despair!

Soon this fallen angel mounts a tower and raises his fist and addresses the world. He claims that he is the one who will create God. He laments the fact that a schism has too long divided evil from good. And he asks if it isn't true that we, the talented artists, haven't made of our work "the only and same virtue?"

These honeyed words are false and a frightful thunderbolt brings the song to an end and kills this wizard who knew how to blend malice and artifice into a lying form of pride.

After the death of the evil angel, the whole tone of the poem changes (Verlaine rewrote this part several times). In some of his most hushed and beautiful lines he describes the enchanted, peaceful countryside, as if he is putting behind the agitated evils of Paris and London and recalling the silent nights of the Ardennes. We are told about "the evangelical countryside, severe and sweet" and the "cold streams coursing over a bed of stones" and the owl "flying through the air balmy with mystery and prayer." The poem ends with an invocation to "the Clement God who protects us from evil." What is remarkable here is that Verlaine, while using Rimbaud's own meter, denounces his lover with Miltonic majesty and then reabsorbs him into the misty, chilly countryside that gave birth to him.

Verlaine was embarked on an experiment in self-renewal. He was composing a book of poems that would eventually be called *Wisdom*, for which he would write some of the most moving and convincing Catholic poems in the French language. Mystical (or moral) experiences are never easy to render. Of course great poets of the late Middle Ages—Dante, Saint John of the Cross, the Sufi poet Rumi—turned out sublime hymns to God, but they were living in an age of faith when doubters were burned alive and religion was the paramount fact of a painful earthly existence. Verlaine, by contrast, was writing about his own troubled faith in an age of supreme skepticism subject to the inquiries of science and demystifying textual scholarship.

Rimbaud himself embraced the spirit of progress and science that characterized his century, although in *A Season in Hell* there is enough Christian language to lend some substance to later critical claims that he, too, was a Catholic poet. Perhaps those same critics have been less ready to acknowledge the essential impiety of the title, which suggests that hell is finite and not eternal, seasonal and not everlasting.

"My fate depends on this book," Rimbaud told his friend Delahaye. Rimbaud's mother, surprisingly, agreed to pay for the publication of the poem, though she scarcely knew what to make of it. Rimbaud sent it off to a Brussels printer, Jacques Poot, who usually published legal journals. By the time of Rimbaud's nineteenth birthday on October 20, 1873, the printing job had been finished. He traveled to Brussels to collect his author's copies. He took about ten, deposited one at Verlaine's prison for him and departed for Paris. There he handed out seven copies to his few remaining friends—none of whom had any celebrity or clout. The important poets he'd met through Verlaine now shunned him, holding him responsible for the terrible fate that had befallen Verlaine. People saw Rimbaud as a hooligan and a pervert who had ruined a talented and previously upstanding married man. Certainly no one wanted to advance the career of such an enemy of art. Rimbaud limped back to Charleville and seems to have lost all interest in his book. He never paid off the remaining fees due to the printer. The other 490 copies of *A Season in Hell* would wait in Monsieur Poot's storeroom until 1901—nearly thirty years later—when they were discovered by a book-lover.

Verlaine, who was about to be transferred to a high-security prison, managed to write three or four poems for Rimbaud by dipping a small stick in prison coffee and scribbling on contraband paper. The "*Crimen Amoris*" was written out this way and given to Arthur. Both of them wrote a few more poems in their private eleven-syllable lines—and then neither ever used the unusual measure again.

Disappointed as a literary contender, and shocked and feeling bereft because of Verlaine's fate, Rimbaud returned quietly to Paris. There he was a social pariah: no one would sit at his table in the cafés he frequented. He had only three or four friends—and a new acquaintance, Germain Nouveau, an unknown poet who had originally moved to Paris from Provence. Nouveau, three years older than Rimbaud, had lost his mother when he was eight and his father when he was twelve—and now was quickly exhausting his small inheritance in a classic bohemian life of dissipation. Nouveau was less than five feet tall and had thick black hair pulled behind his ears and a curly beard that ended in two points—and startlingly intense, dark eyes. His heavy Provençal accent made people smile. He instantly came under the spell of Rimbaud (which troubled his few friends), and almost immediately the two young men decided to leave Paris together for London.

Was Nouveau homosexual and in love with Rimbaud? He'd had an affair with a woman shortly before meeting Rimbaud, but much later he wrote a strangely ambiguous poem called "The Refusal"—a half-humorous, fairly obscure, certainly playful exercise that begins by announcing, "I am a pederast in my soul," but ends in the declaration, "I am not a pederast." In between, the poet muses on the experience of living surrounded by suspicions, an infamy that poisons friendship: "Friendship, this beautiful bitch / That howls at its moon of love." Nouveau describes the founder of the school of pederasty, a movement that doesn't count very many adherents. The founder's name, we're told, rhymes with veau or "veal" (of course it could be Rimbaud or Nouveau). After he tells us that almost all of humanity subscribes to heterosexuality, he mentions there is one exception—presumably Rimbaud, though to pronounce his name would offend the "chaste ears" of the lady to whom the whole poem is addressed. In one other strange passage, Nouveau remarks that since he is "only half a man" (a reference to his short stature), doesn't he have the right to search out someone who would complete him?

Years later Nouveau's friend Jean Richepin recalled that at that time Rimbaud was much better known for his infamous character than for his poems and that his strong personality gained an easy ascendancy over Nouveau, who had "a feeble nature, an exalted character, with the nervousness of a sensual woman abandoning herself to a strong man." To Richepin the departure of Nouveau with Rimbaud for London amounted to an abduction.

Nouveau was an unstable man with a visionary turn of mind. In later years he met Verlaine, who converted him to Catholicism. Nouveau subsequently had such profound mystical experiences that he had to be hospitalized more than once (alcoholism also played its deleterious role in his "visions"); he eventually died from overzealous fasting during Lent. As a middle-aged man, Nouveau would beg in front of a church in Aix-en-Provence. Cezanne, who had known him as a painter and poet in Paris thirty years earlier, would give him a coin every Sunday. By then Nouveau would be calling himself "Humilis" and be violently opposed to the publication of his own poems. He would even sue one publisher who attempted to bring them out.

In London with Rimbaud, Nouveau found great meaning in *Illuminations*, Rimbaud's book of prose poems, and Nouveau copied them out in his own clear hand. The two shared a room together in London near the Waterloo Station, and they joined forces to give an Englishman lessons in French conversation. Both signed up to work at the British Library. Nouveau's letters about London to friends back in Paris sounded disturbingly like those Verlaine had once written; people worried that Rimbaud might ruin Nouveau as well.

Rimbaud had undoubtedly been writing *Illuminations* over many months, but it was at this time that he began assembling and polishing the manuscript. Few of the prose poems in it are longer than two or three pages. They appear to have little or no autobiographical relevance. Many of them refer to painting, an innovation in Rimbaud's work—perhaps due to the influence of living with Germain Nouveau, who was both a poet and a painter. Unlike the sections in *A Season in Hell*, the poems in *Illuminations* do not proceed through the seesaw of thesis and antithesis, nor are they animated by a half-submerged debate. In this new work there is nothing conversational, nothing that suggests contention and revision, statement and counter-statement.

The first poem, "After the Flood," sets the proto-surrealist tone. In the aftermath of the flood, beavers are building a dam and Madame "establishes a piano in the Alps." Caravans take their leave and "the Splendide-Hotel was built in the chaos of glaciers and the polar night." In the next poem, "Childhood," nothing from Rimbaud's own past creeps in. It's all about sultanas and princesses, religious pilgrims and "little foreigners and persons who are sweetly unhappy." In addition, "There is a clock that doesn't ring" and "a cathedral that descends and a lake that rises up"—a reference to the old legend of the "drowned cathedral."

In "Tale," a prince "merges" with a genie whose looks and bearing promise "a multiple and complex love" and "an unspeakable—even intolerable—happiness." In "Antique," Rimbaud invokes a gracious son of the god Pan. "Your heart," he writes, "beats in your stomach where a double sex sleeps. Stroll about by night, softly moving this thigh, this second thigh and this left leg." These lines have become celebrated as the essence of Rimbaud's final style and in French they are unforgettable: "*Promène-toi, la nuit, en mouvant cette cuisse, cette seconde cuisse et cette jambe de gauche.*" The words suggest a highly stylized tableau, like Nijinski's later choreography in profile for Debussy's *The Afternoon of a Faun.*

In other poems Rimbaud celebrates departures in which the goal is to attain new affections, or he calls for the rebirth of sensuality: "Our bones are clothed in a new loving body." He writes of "new harmony" and "new men" and "the new love." There are almost Gnostic utterances: "We know how to give all our life every single day."

Most of the book, however, is icy and futuristic— meditations on cities of crystal with boulevards where poor young families nourish themselves on fruit. In another city, a short bridge leads to a big dome described as "an armature of artistic steel fifteen thousand feet in diameter more or less." The strange turns of language, of fairy-tale grandeur and precision-tooled sizes—this is the side of Rimbaud that appealed to the Surrealists. Whereas later critics felt they had sucked all the juice out of Verlaine and perfectly digested him, Rimbaud remained somehow…inedible. He was impossible to assimilate and therefore remained endlessly fascinating for future generations of poets and exegetes.

Many of the poems contain English words, place names or odd anglicisms (the mistakes a native speaker would make in French). The various English words include "steerage," "turf," "Cottage," "Pier," "Railways." It was obvious that Rimbaud was immersed in English at the time he was composing the poems, though exactly when is not clear. He would live in London four times altogether, spending a total of eleven months there. From this last period we have a long list in Rimbaud's hand of unusual English words he'd compiled to study.

Two of the poems included in *Illuminations* are sometimes said to be the first examples of free verse in French—that is, irregular, unmetered, and unrhymed lines (perhaps translations into modern European languages of the Biblical Psalms are the origin of all free verse). The free-verse poems are called "Marine" and "Movement." Both are about the motion of the sea, and "Movement" has a strangely modern sound. Here is the second stanza of this weird tale of a futuristic Noah's Ark:

They are the conquerors of the world
Seeking a personal chemical fortune;
Sport and comfort travel with them.
They are the leaders of
Races, classes and animals climbing into the Ship.
Rest and dizziness exist
In the diluvian light
Of terrifying nights of study.

The title *Illuminations* was never written anywhere by Rimbaud and may have been a coinage of Verlaine's, who saw the poems into print. According to his notes (and owing to his often faulty English), Verlaine thought the word meant "colored plates," though perhaps he— or Rimbaud—had in mind something like the spiritual illuminations of Swedenborg. Rimbaud had studied the works of the Swedish mystic and for a while lived next door to a Swedenborgian church in London. Or perhaps the title referred to something like moments of sudden inspiration.

According to the great twentieth-century French poet, Yves Bonnefoy, the last poem in the collection, "Genie," is "one of the most beautiful poems of our language," a sentiment echoed by the translator and critic Roger

Munier, who has written, "'Genie' is more than a poem. It is an inspired text, worthy of being counted among the great texts that we label 'canonical' in a world such as ours, which comes after the retreat of the gods." Munier's point is understandable, for the genie is not a god, though it seems partly divine and partly human (and also partly animal and partly robotic). Touched with god-like powers, but of a restricted, local sort. Exalted but remote. Eternal but crossing our world no more often than a meteor....

To be sure, to call it the "last" poem is misleading, since the poems have never been published in any definitive or particular order and Rimbaud's intentions were unclear. Certainly the strange superimpositions of visual imagery in the poems suggest the act of laying one slide on top of another and looking at the resulting combinations—"an arm of the sea, without boats...between docks loaded with gigantic candelabras" is a typical superimposition.

What is extraordinary is that in his brief writing career Rimbaud covered the whole history of poetry from Latin verse up through the Romantics and the Parnassians and the Symbolists on to the Surrealists, even before surrealism existed.

Like most of the poems in *Illuminations*, "Genie" is shadowy, dreamlike, inspiring, indecipherable:

He is affection and exists in the present since he has declared open house to foamy winter and the sound of summer, he who has purified drinks and foods, he who is the spell cast over elusive places and is the superhuman pleasure attached to those sites that are stationary. He is affection and the future, the strength and love that we, mired in our fury and boredom, see rush overhead in an angry tempest through flags of ecstasy.

He is love, cut to a perfect and reinvented size, he is reason, miraculous and unforeseen, and he is eternity: a beloved machine of fatal attractions. We have all been terrified by his concessions—his and ours: oh the pleasure of our health, the play of our faculties, our self-serving affection and passion for him, he who will love us down through the long years of his infinite life....

We call him back to us but he moves on....And if Adoration goes away, rings, then his promise also rings forth: "Put behind you these superstitions, these former bodies, these families and these generations. It is this whole era that has gone under!"

He will not go away, he will not come down again from heaven, he won't manage to redeem angry women or merry men nor all this sin: for there's no more to say since he exists and is beloved.

His breaths, his heads, his marathons; the terrifying swiftness of his perfect shape and movement.

O the fertility of his mind and the immensity of the universe!

His body! The dreamed-of detachment, the dissolution of grace crossed with new violence!

The look of him! The look! When he saunters past, all humiliating sufferings are lifted.

His light! Music most intense drowns out all the groans of suffering in motion.

His step! Migrations vaster than the ancient invasions.

Hail to him and us! A pride more benign than all lost good deeds.

O world! And the soft song of new unhappiness!

He has known all of us and loved us all. Let us salute him this winter night and watch him as he swerves from cape to cape, from the stormy pole to the castle, from the crowd to the beach, from one glance to another, his energy and feelings spent, and let us dismiss him, sending him under the tides and onto the peaks of a snowy desert as we follow his looks, his body, his light.

Germain Nouveau left Rimbaud in London in June, not with a violent rupture but nonetheless definitively. He remained loyal to Rimbaud, however, as an artist. Later Rimbaud handed Verlaine the manuscript of *Illuminations* with the idea that he in turn would give the prose poems to Nouveau, who had promised to see them into print. As it turned out, they were not published for another decade, over several issues of a literary magazine called *La Vogue*, coming out in fortnightly installments between May 13 and June 21, 1886. They were ascribed to "the late Arthur Rimbaud." The poet, of course, was still alive, but no one had heard from him in some time. When they appeared in book form (with a laudatory introduction by Verlaine), Rimbaud was being hailed as a precursor of the Symbolists. Félix Fénéon wrote in a review that the *Illuminations* were "images of distant civilizations from a bygone epic or an industrial future." From our present perspective, the "industrial future" looks like the safer bet.

On his own in London, Rimbaud felt ostracized by the French community in exile there. Even the slightly mad and very bohemian Nouveau prudently had referred to Rimbaud not by name but simply as "Thing" ("*Chose*")—which later became a half-affectionate, half-derogatory reference in gay slang in English ("Miss Thing!").

In June 1874 Rimbaud fell ill and had to be hospitalized in London. Nothing is known about the nature of his illness, but it was the first of many. Whatever it was, the disease was sufficiently serious for Rimbaud to call on his mother's help. Madame Rimbaud and his sister Vitalie made the trip from the Ardennes to London and arrived on July 6. Arthur had engaged a large room for them on Argyle Square at one end of Euston Road. In her journal, Vitalie wrote in her best little-girl manner: "He is thin and pale, but he's much better and his great delight in seeing us will hasten his complete recovery. Despite the confusion when we were getting off the train, he saw us immediately and came up to us...."

For the next twenty-six days, Rimbaud translated for his mother and sister and took them on constant tours of the city to such sights as the Tower, the Houses of

Parliament, Buckingham Palace, Trafalgar Square, the Albert Memorial, Saint Paul's Cathedral, and even the pedestrian tube under the Thames, the "Thames Subway." Vitalie, the typical backward country girl, hated London and was filled with homesickness. She knew that her mother didn't want to return to France before Arthur's health was entirely restored and he'd found a "position." After this visit Arthur was definitively reconciled with Madame Rimbaud and in the coming years would depend on her more and more. He would pass many winter months with her, help her take in the harvest in the fall, and correspond with her frequently no matter where his journeys took him.

Rimbaud found a job—the first in his life. And yet where it was and what it was exactly remain wrapped in mystery. One theory holds that it was teaching French in a school in Scotland—or perhaps in Reading. In any event the period between July 31 and November 7, 1874, remains unclear. On November 7 and for the next two days, Rimbaud ran an advertisement in the Times:

A PARISIAN (20) of high literary and linguistic attainments, excellent conversation, will be glad to ACCOMPAGNY a GENTLEMAN (artists preferred), or a family wishing to travel in southern or eastern countries. Good references.—A. R., no 165, King's Road, Reading.

Nothing came of the announcement. All it indicated was Rimbaud's intense desire to travel. Gentlemen artists (if they existed) probably had no need of a twenty-year-old conversationalist as they toured Bulgaria or Greece.

During the next four years, from 1875 on, Rimbaud took long trips throughout Europe and even farther. He seems to have had an idea that he could become fluent in several languages and work eventually as an interpreter in commerce. At twenty-one he evidenced a strong urge to change his life entirely—and to avoid the literary world where he'd earned nothing but a detestable reputation. We think of him as a powerful and successful poet, and yet he thought of himself as a failure. He had interrupted his studies and had never won the general certificate of education needed to teach in the French school system. In Paris he was widely known as a thug and a troublemaker—and above all a homosexual. Scandal followed him wherever he went. Twelve or fifteen years would have to go by before the Paris literary world would be willing to admit that Rimbaud was the father of modern poetry. One wonders if he could ever have occupied that exalted position if he'd gone on living—and living in France.

What must be underlined is that Rimbaud had bade farewell forever to literature. He didn't write it and he didn't even read it from now on till the end of his life. He looked back on his years of creativity (from age fifteen to nineteen) as shameful, a time of drunkenness, a period of homosexual scandal, of arrogance and rebellion that led to nothing. He was desperate to be a success—at anything, more or less. First he tried poetry and abandoned it when he could get no one to look at *A Season in Hell*. He then tried learning languages, which he would use as a traveler, a businessman, an interpreter. He tried to turn himself into a pianist—and gave that up quickly. He had no bona fide skills—just genius, which no one seemed to appreciate—so he turned to gunrunning, dealing in import-export, exploration, and writing about it (but in the driest possible way). Since he'd failed as a writer he rejected all bohemian values and longed for the sort of respectability and financial gain that his mother would admire.

In January 1875 Rimbaud stayed with his mother in Charleville and applied himself to the study of German. On February 13 he left by train for Stuttgart with a small allowance from her. He was going to learn German in Germany. As he had in London, he ran an advertisement offering French lessons but again there were no takers.

Rimbaud had an unexpected visitor—Verlaine—who had just been freed from prison and expelled from Belgium. After spending a few days with his mother in their village Verlaine had traveled to Paris, where he attempted in vain to see his wife, whose divorce had finally gone through. Since Mathilde refused him, Verlaine next sought out Rimbaud.

Verlaine made a great show of his recent conversion to Catholicism and of his newly pious ways; even before Rimbaud saw him he was referring contemptuously to Verlaine as "Loyola" (after the founder of the Jesuits) in letters to mutual friends. At the end of February, Rimbaud and Verlaine spent two and a half days together in Stuttgart. Rimbaud led the newly pious Verlaine into many German drinking places—and soon the apostle was roaring drunk. But he had already put aside his sacred airs. As Rimbaud wrote to their mutual friend Delahaye: "Verlaine arrived here the other day, a rosary in his claws....Three hours later he had denied his god and made the 98 wounds of Our Lord bleed again. He stayed two and a half days, very reasonable, and following my remonstrations he has returned to Paris in order to go on to study over there on the island." Indeed, by March 20, Verlaine had taken up a post as teacher of French and drawing in England in a grammar school in Stickney, Lincolnshire.

Verlaine and Rimbaud never saw each other again, though in other ways they remained in each other's lives. Verlaine still cared enough about Rimbaud to be jealous. He was especially curious about the miniscule Germain Nouveau and arranged a meeting with him in London, where the two poets got drunk and no doubt exchanged reminiscences about "Thing." By now Verlaine's reputation was at an all-time low, and when he submitted poems hoping they would be included in an anthology of Parnassian poets, the editor rejected them immediately, saying, "The author is unworthy."

After spending two and a half months in Stuttgart, Rimbaud set off on a trip with Italy as his new destination; he was determined to learn Italian but was so poor that he had to walk over the St. Gotthard Pass in Switzerland. He arrived, exhausted, in Milan, where he lodged with a widow in a house facing the cathedral. The other residents of the house were a colorful assortment of cooks, rag merchants, laborers, and tailors. To thank the widow for her hospitality, Rimbaud gave her a copy of *A Season in Hell*—the last time we see him showing any interest in his poetic work whatsoever.

His next stop was Marseille. Rimbaud was planning to travel on to Spain in order to pick up another language, but he fell ill and spent some time in a Marseille hospital—perhaps the very one where he would die sixteen years later. When a friend ran into Rimbaud in Marseille, the ex-poet claimed that he was living by stealing and had even seduced a monk in order to get free room and board in the monastery. Soon Verlaine and Delahaye, Rimbaud's childhood friend, had gotten hold of this bit of gossip; Delahaye wrote to Verlaine with a cartoon showing Rimbaud with a tear in his eye appealing to an enormously fat monk. In any event Rimbaud gave up his project to visit Spain.

It would be satisfying to think that Rimbaud and Verlaine, though no longer lovers, remained on distantly amicable terms. But in fact Rimbaud kept trying to milk Verlaine for money, as he'd always done. Rimbaud even threatened to blackmail his former paramour. In a letter to Delahaye, Verlaine complained of Rimbaud's "stupid ingratitude," his rudeness, his "impertinence augmented by dark hints of blackmail." Later, when Verlaine and Delahaye championed Rimbaud's writing and presented him to the world as a precocious genius, they had long since put behind them the gossipy, nasty tone of their letters of this period.

Rimbaud returned to his mother's house in Charleville. His little sister Vitalie was suffering from cancer. Rimbaud, bored witless, decided he wanted to be a pianist and ordered a piano to be delivered to the family home; soon the outraged neighbors were complaining of the noise. Then Rimbaud announced he wanted to study the sciences and hoped to pass the high-school diploma he'd once scorned, but planning this time to take it in science—a scheme that came to nothing. Delahaye, shocked by the amount of drink that Rimbaud was putting away, confided to Verlaine that he thought their friend, "Thing," was destined for the madhouse. Verlaine, always a quick study, wrote reams of doggerel in his letters to Delahaye in which he versified all the latest news about "Rimbe." In one burlesque poem he wrote:

The curse of never being tired
Dogs your steps across the world as the horizon
  beckons,
You, the prodigal son who gestures like a satyr!

Farther down in the same poem Verlaine added:

You're no longer up to anything decent: your
  language
Is dead from too much slang and sneering
And from working up the lies of the moment.
Your memory, stopped up with obscenities,
Can no longer hold on to the merest idea…
Oh God of the meek, save this child from anger!

To go along with his new image as pianist-scientist, perhaps, Rimbaud shaved his head down to the skull—this glorious hair that he had grown long in his heyday and nurtured as a nest for lice. Now he complained of constant headaches and thought that getting rid of his thick cowlicky hair would solve the problem.

Verlaine wrote Rimbaud his last letter on December 12, 1875. He still refused to give the younger man his address for fear he'd blackmail him or cause some other sort of trouble. He didn't want to subsidize Rimbaud. Nor could he resist suggesting that Rimbaud was ready to return to the Catholic faith: "It's so grievous to see you going in such an idiotic direction, you who are so intelligent, so ready (though it would astonish you to admit it!). I challenge your very disgust with everything and everyone, your constant anger against every single thing—well-founded, this anger, though you don't understand why." Ever optimistic, Verlaine saw the beginnings of a religious vocation even in Rimbaud's constant irritation and rage. The two men had reached a low point; as Rimbaud's best French biographer Jean-Jacques Lefrère puts it: "In Verlaine's eyes, Rimbaud had become a master blackmailer and an ingrate. For Rimbaud, Verlaine was only a reluctant source of funds and a hypocritical Jesuit."

On December 18 Rimbaud's sister Vitalie died at age seventeen, probably of a tubercular tumor on the knee ("tubercular synovitis" was the diagnosis of the day) Rimbaud had always been fond of her; she had been the one who'd visited him in London and to whom he was always bringing home little gifts.

Tired of science and the piano, Rimbaud now turned to Russian. He had a scheme to visit Russia and in order to master its language he would lock himself away in an armoire, without food or drink, sometimes for twenty-four hours at a stretch as he perused a Russian dictionary. He who had once been so violently anticlerical now toyed with the idea of becoming a missionary so that he could be sent free to distant climes. He actually set off for Russia but only made it as far as Vienna, where he was robbed and beaten by a coachman and sent limping home to his mother.

Soon he was in Brussels again, joining the Dutch navy and being shipped out as a recruit to Sumatra and eventually to Java, where he deserted a month after his arrival. He boarded an English ship, the *Wandering*

Chief, survived a storm on the Cape of Good Hope, and landed in Ireland, whence he made his way back to Charleville and his mother's side. Why did Rimbaud make this long and futile trip? Partly for the bonus, no doubt, paid by the Dutch government—the equivalent of a tradesman's annual salary. But mostly for the pleasure of travel. Rimbaud longed to travel, and once it was in his blood that was all he could dream of doing. Later he even considered marrying, but he stipulated to his matchmaker—his mother—that he would need a wife willing to follow him to far-flung places since he was incapable of a sedentary life.

The next two years, 1877 and 1878, are among the most mysterious in Rimbaud's life. He had sought employment in America but failed to find a position. He traveled to Copenhagen and Stockholm, where he sold tickets for a French circus. Then he was off to Marseille, where he boarded a ship bound for Alexandria but had to be put ashore in Italy because he'd fallen ill with a gastrointestinal fever. The Italian doctor said that due to excessive walking his ribs had worn through the walls of his abdomen—which, far-fetched as it might sound, was entirely likely, given that Rimbaud had walked not once but twice from the Ardennes down through the Alps and into Italy. Each time Rimbaud came back to Charleville, his old friends noticed that he was a bit more withdrawn and silent, as if he'd already broken definitively with them and Europe.

On October 20, the day he turned twenty-four, Rimbaud left Charleville with the intention of traveling to Egypt. He spent two weeks in Alexandria—and then shipped out to Cyprus, where he was the foreman overseeing a team of twenty stoneworkers in a quarry. There his men used dynamite to break up stone deposits and then collect the debris. By May 1878, six months after starting work in Cyprus, Rimbaud was heading home with a fever and weak lungs. The doctor his mother engaged diagnosed typhoid and malaria. His old friend Delahaye was struck by the physical changes in Rimbaud—the hollow cheeks, the sparse blond beard, the deep, calm voice. When Delahaye asked him if he was still writing poetry, Rimbaud looked half-annoyed, half-amused, as if he'd been asked if he still played with hoops, and replied, "I'm no longer concerned with that." When a year later one of his friends in Charleville boasted of just having bought several books of poetry, Rimbaud muttered that such books served no function except to hide the cracks in the wall.

In 1880 Rimbaud returned for two months to work in Cyprus, but he left his job after a dispute with his boss. This time, however, he did not come home to the Ardennes but went to Egypt instead. He was looking for work of some sort in a Red Sea port. A Frenchman he met along the way suggested he go on to Aden, the leading port town in southwestern Arabia, in present-day Yemen. Rimbaud arrived there during the first half of August 1880, and this move would open the next and final chapter in his life. For the next decade he would live and work in Africa until his death in France in 1891.

Rimbaud fell sick as soon as he arrived in Aden. It was intolerably hot. The principal town, called Crater, was trapped in the crater of an extinct volcano. It rained there only once a year and most of the drinking water came from distilling seawater. Rimbaud was hired to grade and sort coffee beans; Aden was a collecting point for such regional products as coffee, ivory, ostrich plumes, gold, pearls, and animal skins as well as various spices and incense. When he started working, he had only seven francs to his name. He wrote his mother (for the first time in two months) and told her that as soon as he'd saved a few hundred francs he'd head for the nearly mythical island of Zanzibar; over the years he would mention Zanzibar over and over as his dream destination, always adding, "There's a lot of work down there."

Much of the information we have about Rimbaud's decade in Arabia and North Africa comes from his letters to his mother and surviving sister. These letters are invariably complaining and grim. "Aden is a rock," he wrote, "dreadful, without a single leaf of grass or a drop of good water (people drink distilled seawater). The heat is excessive, especially in June and September, which are both subject to heat waves. Ninety-five is the usual temperature night and day in an office that is very cool and well ventilated. Everything is very expensive—and so on. There's nothing to do about it; I'm like a prisoner here and I'll certainly have to stick it out at least three months before I can get back on my feet and find a better job."

In his next letter, Rimbaud couldn't help but get in a jab about home while still complaining about his present circumstances: "Aden as everyone admits is the most tedious place on earth except for the one where you live."

His new boss, Alfred Bardey, a fellow Frenchman, described Rimbaud in a letter to an associate: "He's a tall and pleasant guy who seldom speaks and accompanies his brief explanations with little choppy, irregular gestures of his right hand." Bardey noted that Rimbaud already spoke enough Arabic to win the esteem of his native coworkers, though they called him "Karani," the Arab word for "bad" or "nasty," a name they gave to all the lower-ranking Europeans. Bardey didn't look too closely into Rimbaud's past; he was favorably enough impressed by his aura of being a frank and upright man.

Although Rimbaud had turned his back squarely on literature, he remained obsessed with books. Like the two touching but absurd autodidacts in Flaubert's *Bouvard et Pecuchet*, his "tragic-comic novel," Rimbaud wanted to learn everything in every domain of practical knowledge. He ordered books from France on metallurgy, hydraulics, operating a steamship, naval architecture, mineralogy, how to set up a lumber yard, a pocket guide to carpentry, masonry, and so on. He ordered *The New Manual for Cartwrights and Carriage-Builders*, *The Glassmaker's Manual*, manuals on brick-making, foundries, candle-making, porcelain-making, house-painting, and telegraphy. In his grandiosity and inclusiveness, he ordered an instruction book, *The Commander of Steam-Ships*. He who had hoped to reshape the world through the alchemy of language was now reduced to the study of actual practical techniques. And yet the goal—to know everything and control everything—remained the same.

Rimbaud's new company sent him off to Harar, a high-walled town in the mountains about five hundred miles from Addis Ababa, the capital of modern Ethiopia. In Rimbaud's time, Harar had just come under Egyptian domination, and the region was controlled by a barracks full of Sudanese soldiers under Egyptian leadership. It was considered the fourth holiest city in Islam after Mecca, Medina, and Jerusalem. Harar was a twenty days' trip by donkey or horse across a burning desert from the coastal town of Zeila on the Red Sea. Camels were used just to carry goods. Each of the tribesmen who were paid to accompany him wore the testicles of his enemies in his headdress (fifty years later the Abyssinians would castrate dozens of Mussolini's soldiers and decorate a triumphal arch with these sacs—and take a photograph of it, which they sent to Il Duce).

The temperature of Harar itself was relatively cool due to the high altitude. The town was surrounded by walls ten feet tall, which protected the villagers from lions and leopards. Sometimes hyenas would wriggle in through breaches in the mud wall to devour the sick and invalid who lived in the streets. Harar—not to be confused with the capital of Zimbabwe, Harare—had 30,000 inhabitants. As a sacred Muslim site (with its nearly one hundred mosques), until recently it had been forbidden to Europeans; in 1854 Sir Richard Francis Burton was the first Christian to enter it, disguised as an Arab merchant. The town, having no sewers, smelled. It was famous for its horse market. Harar was also known for coffee, which the locals drank like tea, infused in hot water. Rimbaud, a diligent and gifted linguist, not only already could bargain in Arabic, but soon learned the local languages of Harari and Oromo. When he went out on caravans he dressed as an Arab merchant and covered his head; he had no trouble passing, though his startling blue eyes might have been a giveaway. The house that tourist guides now point out as Rimbaud's was in fact built after his death. The decrepit "palace" where Rimbaud actually lived and worked—long since demolished—was at the time the only two-story structure in town. It had once been the local pasha's residence.

Rimbaud kept the account books for his company, weighed the sacks of coffee, and paid the local coffee brokers. His company also bought ivory and animal skins. Although Rimbaud was living in an ancient walled town menaced by lions and reachable only by desert caravan, and though he was awakened by the call of muezzins and was dealing in ivory tusks, in his letters home he made nothing of all this exoticism. In *A Season in Hell*, he had longed for far-flung places; he had written, "I am seated, a leper, on broken pots and nettles, at the foot of a wall eaten away by the sun." Now that his "dream" had come true, perhaps he was sobered by its stark reality. Or perhaps he felt no need to comment on it in letters to his dry-eyed mother, who respected nothing but a solid character, hard work, and money. More in Rimbaud's new style was a letter to a maker of precision instruments in Paris: "I want to know everything about what is the best equipment manufactured in France (or abroad) for mathematics, mechanics, astronomy, electricity, meteorology...."

Rimbaud was only twenty-six, but he seemed to have put behind him his transgressive behavior, his drunkenness, his love of poetry and literature, his creativity, his homosexuality, even most of his arrogance. There is some evidence that he contracted syphilis in a Harar whorehouse. He wrote his mother: "I've picked up an illness that isn't serious in itself but this climate is treacherous for every kind of illness." Soon he was complaining that once he'd saved some money he would leave Harar, "for if you suppose that I'm living like a prince, for my part I'm certain that I live in a manner that is stupid and annoying." He asked his mother to root around in his father's papers and find the folder his father had put together of Arab jokes and puns. His father, after two decades of living apart from his family, had died in Dijon on November 17, 1878—an event the family letters don't even mention until three months later, when there is a document to sign regarding the inheritance. Captain Rimbaud had never been part of his family's life. His son Arthur, who hadn't seen him since age six, shared his love of travel and his fascination with other cultures and languages, but there all resemblance stopped.

Rimbaud kept longing to go off on his own, to lead an expedition or caravan of his own devising—from which all the profits would accrue to him. In fact his dreams during these years were to go to Zanzibar, to marry a nice girl from the Ardennes who would be willing to live in Africa, to have a son he could raise as an engineer—and to become rich from African trading. Not one of these dreams was ever realized. No wonder his letters home were always so morose. In one he told his mother, "It would be unfortunate at your age to have to work. Alas, I'm not at all partial to living; and if I live I'm accustomed to going around being exhausted; but if I'm forced to go on exhausting myself like this and to be worn down by worries as wrenching as they are absurd in this atrocious climate, I'm afraid I'll shorten my existence....I want to start a little bit of business of my own, for I don't want to spend my whole life in slavery here."

Before he could lead his own caravan, he needed to go on working for Bardey. On one fifteen-day expedition, he and a Greek merchant set out due south for Boubassa— they were the first Europeans to explore this part of the world. Rimbaud became ill for several weeks with high fevers, and his companion's horse was devoured by a lion. Nor did the caravan make a profit.

Back in Harar, there was a sudden outbreak of typhus. Every morning twenty people had died (twice as many if it rained). The cadavers were put outside the walls where the hyenas and vultures picked the bones clean. When his mother complained that he seldom wrote and obviously was forgetting her, Rimbaud replied: "But I think of you and nothing but you. What should I say about my work here, which already repulses me so much, or about this country, which horrifies me?" In the next letter he continued his threnody: "The climate is bad-tempered and humid; the work I do is ridiculous and stupefying." When Rimbaud was promoted he wrote to his mother: "If you need anything take some of my money, it's yours. I have no one to worry about except myself, and I have need of very little."

After a year in Harar, Rimbaud was called back to Aden by his boss—just in time for a cholera epidemic. There he learned in a letter from his mother that the question of his military service in France was still pending. Every young man in France was obliged to serve in the army at some point. Rimbaud had never done his service, a problem he now worried over incessantly and would in fact still be fretting about on his deathbed. As it turned out, his brother Frédéric's military service exempted him.

While Rimbaud was sweating and suffering from boredom in Africa and struggling to establish his fortune and good character, his fame as a poet was beginning to grow back in France—mainly due to the efforts of Verlaine. When his childhood friend Delahaye wrote him to this effect, Rimbaud could only respond with a fairly formal letter asking him to send him surveying equipment so that he, Rimbaud, could submit a scholarly paper on the geography of Harar and the surrounding region. (In his next letter to this faithful friend, Rimbaud mistakenly calls Delahaye Alfred instead of Ernest.) Although his links with the Ardennes were broken, his mother invested some of his money in a few acres there adjacent to the family farm.

In his complaining letters, Rimbaud sometimes comments curiously on his own ill humor: "I hope to be able to find some rest before I die. Of course now I'm used to all sorts of trials and if I complain, it's a kind of singing." The "Tedium Bird" is what one might call Rimbaud at this point in his life.

For once, his activities fall into a regular pattern. He masters languages with a true gift and assiduity. He leads a sober, self-effacing life and seems genuinely proud of making a favorable impression on his European colleagues and employers. When he hears that his wastrel brother Frédéric had considered bringing up Rimbaud's homosexual past in order to blackmail him, Rimbaud replies to his mother: "That doesn't surprise me about Frédéric: he's a complete idiot, as we've always known, and we were always full of admiration for his empty head." Later Rimbaud wrote defensively: "Nobody in Aden can say anything against me. On the contrary. For the last ten years everyone here has thought well of me. A word to the wise!" Despite his developing desire to seem like a good solid person, Rimbaud could not resist making scornful remarks about the people around him. He struck most observers as silent and angry and unhappy, and even referred to himself as "bizarre." Once in Aden he slapped a local merchant whom he accused of insolence, an incident that aroused the ire of the other Arabs.

Rimbaud had nothing but scorn for his previous Parisian literary life. When his boss Bardey, for instance, asked him about his time in London, he dismissed it as "a period of drunkenness." And when another curious colleague in Africa asked him about his career as a poet, Rimbaud said, "Hogwash—it was only hogwash." The word in French he used was *rinçures*, an unusual one that comes from the word for "rinsing" and means "dishwater" or "slops," and is even used for "bad wine." Whereas "hogwash" sounds blustery and dated to our ears, *rinçures* is suitably strange and sticks in the mind.

In Africa, all Rimbaud wanted to do was to make money, though he directed some of his energy to scientific or practical activities. In February 1884, he published a paper in the journal of a geographical society on his trip through the Ogadine; the paper, which was read out loud to the Société de Géographie, was considered useful despite its "dryness." In another quasi-scientific venture, Rimbaud bought the equipment necessary for taking and developing photographs. His pictures, all a bit blurry, include three self-portraits in which he is dressed in baggy, off-white cotton clothes. He looks thin, lined, and much older. Nothing of the boyish angel remains.

He hired a male servant, Djami, who stayed with him for seven years and to whom Rimbaud left some money. Some people wondered if Djami was Rimbaud's lover, though no evidence points to that conclusion; Djami had a wife and children. He wasn't a slave, though Rimbaud in no way disapproved of slavery (he even once asked a white friend of his to purchase for him two slave boys—a request which the friend rather indignantly refused, advising Rimbaud to abandon the idea altogether). Rimbaud's first English-language biographer, Enid Starkie, cooked up a story that Rimbaud was a slave-trader, twisting the "evidence" to fabricate this legend that still endures. Rimbaud had been a gunrunner but never a slave-trader. Slavery and the slave trade were facts of life in Africa, though none of the slave-traders were white (they were all Arab).

For one year, 1884, Rimbaud lived with an Abyssinian woman in Aden. She seems to have been the only mistress he ever had. One of Rimbaud's acquaintances recalled that she dressed in the European fashion, went out walking with Rimbaud every night, and loved to smoke cigarettes. When Rimbaud left Aden, he sent the Abyssinian woman back to her home with some money. No one knows her name, though a stunning photograph of her exists, in which her young, regular-featured, and rather masculine face is framed in an immaculate white headdress contrasting with her black, matte skin. Was Rimbaud "going native"? One Italian explorer who met him later wrote that Rimbaud lived in a hut, and that when he had to defecate he would squat like the villagers—who, the Italian also reports, "thought of Rimbaud, almost, as a Muslim."

Despite his good standing and his solid position, Rimbaud considered life in Africa "the most atrocious in the world," and he assured his mother that one year there was the equivalent to five years anywhere else. A born complainer, despite his hatred of Africa he did not long for France. No, he'd never be able to tolerate the cold there, he wrote; he would only be able to visit France in the summertime—and in any event, if he was rich enough to travel, then he'd never stay anywhere longer than two months. His mother was equally tragic and unhappy. In a letter complaining that she hasn't heard from Rimbaud in months, she writes, "Your silence is long and why this silence? Happy are those who have no children or who don't love them. They are indifferent to whatever might happen to them."

In 1885 Rimbaud quit his job (in point of fact, his longtime employer Bardey was going out of business) and became an independent merchant. He signed a contract with a certain Pierre Labutut to organize a caravan to deliver guns to Menelik, the forty-three-year-old king of Shewa. Menelik was consolidating various regions, expanding the territory of Abyssinia. He was intent on conquering Harar, Rimbaud's former headquarters; the town would give him access to the Red Sea and preclude the need for crossing the vast, nearly impassable desert. By the end of the century, Menelik would become the first emperor of Abyssinia, his rule internationally recognized (Haile Selassie, the later emperor, was related to Menelik's aunt); and it was no accident that Menelik had taken the name of a Biblical ruler who, according to legend, was the son of Solomon and the Queen of Sheba.

Before setting out on his expedition, Rimbaud waited along the coast in the port of Tadjouri, just north of Djibouti, for a shipment. He received 2,040 rifles and 60,000 Remington cartridges, which he kept in a campsite while organizing a camel caravan—a nearly impossible endeavor, since the local sultan demanded so much bribe money.

After nearly nine months of negotiations and delay, Rimbaud at last prepared to leave the coast for the interior. His associate Labatut had just died from bone cancer. Another business partner, Paul Soleillet, died at the same time of a heart attack induced by a deadly fever—an inauspicious beginning to what turned out to be an ill-fated journey. Rimbaud was about to undertake a fifty-day trip across the hottest and most arid desert in the world, a truly lunar landscape that contained the largest inland salt lake in the world. Few plants grew in the volcanic soil. Rimbaud, along with his hired men and camels, did not arrive in the first village belonging to Menelik until February 6, 1887, after an exhausting four-month tramp.

Although Rimbaud could speak Arabic and two of the languages of Abyssinia (modern Ethiopia), and was tireless and known for his strong will, his sour disposition and perhaps even his contempt for women caused him to make one crucial mistake in diplomacy—refusing to court, or bribe, Menelik's greedy and vengeful wife. As a result, the king announced that Rimbaud's recently deceased business partner, Labatut, had sizable outstanding debts. The king decided to deduct the sum of these putative debts from the money he owed Rimbaud for the arms. When Rimbaud protested that he had signed an agreement with Labatut separating their business dealings, the king ignored it. To make matters worse, Labatut had left behind an Abyssinian widow who now claimed her share of the remaining profits. Once the local merchants saw that the vultures were picking at Rimbaud, other creditors—real or false—stepped forward. The king backed some of their claims, and soon the whole situation was quickly deteriorating for Rimbaud, who eventually limped back to Harar after spending nearly two months in Menelik's capital city of Entotto. Rimbaud announced that after twenty-one months of planning and effort he had lost sixty percent of his capital—surely an exaggeration. It seems that in spite of his losses he'd still managed to turn a considerable profit—though how much no one will ever know, since Rimbaud was so secretive.

Although Rimbaud was only 33, his whole body was becoming more and more tormented with rheumatism. His travails in Abyssinia—and in general his extremely hard life during all his African years—had left him in very rough shape. Perhaps the only sense of accomplishment he derived from his gunrunning trip was an article he published in a French-language newspaper coming out of Alexandria, the *Bosphore Egyptien*. The article—in the form of a letter and not a scientific report—commented on the recent situation in Abyssinia and Harar and recommended that for strategic reasons the French should seize Djibouti—which the French did do just a year later. Since the completion of the Suez Canal in 1869, an invaluable shortcut to the Far East, several major European powers were grabbing land in Africa (a period often called by historians the Scramble for Africa).

Shortly afterward, Rimbaud's old boss Bardey published in the bulletin of the Société géographique an account of Rimbaud's trip from Menelik's capital of Entotto to Harar—a previously unknown route. Rimbaud now wanted to be a journalist, as he'd once planned to be as an adolescent. He sent off articles to various French newspapers without success. At this time he wrote a note to Bardey saying that he did not intend to stay in Harar "because I am used to a free life." He invoked the oft-mentioned chimera of visiting Zanzibar, though nothing came of it.

Once again Rimbaud wrote his mother and sister with his latest lamentations:

> For the past two years my business has been going very badly, I've been wearing myself out uselessly and I have a great deal of difficulty holding on to what I have. I'd like to be done with these satanic countries once and for all; but I keep hoping things will get better and I stay on losing my time in the midst of deprivations and suffering that you can't imagine. And then what would I do in France? It's certain that I could no longer live a sedentary life and above all I'm very much afraid of the cold— and then I don't have sufficient funds, nor a job,

nor outside help, nor connections, nor a profession, nor resources of any sort. If I came back I would be digging my own grave....

Later, he adds, "You must think of me as a new Jeremiah with my perpetual lamentations, but my situation really isn't very cheerful."

Instead of traveling to Zanzibar, Rimbaud decided to work on his own in Harar. Though he insisted he couldn't bear a sedentary life, he would remain in Harar for the next four years and became one of the least peripatetic European merchants in Africa. An Italian visitor described him as wearing extremely simple cotton pajamas of his own design in which he'd done away with the nuisance of buttons. With a Greek friend, Rimbaud would spend long, dull Harari evenings—and at least once a week go out on horseback excursions to nearby points of interest. In his own business Rimbaud was importing cotton, silk, and little manufactured items and was exporting coffee, scents, ivory, and gold. A French businessman said he had never met Rimbaud's like for "correctness and clarity" in the way he kept his books. The local bishop, a Frenchman, described Rimbaud as tall and taciturn, obviously cultivated "but of a secretive and enigmatic nature." Yet another French visitor remembered that Rimbaud had a distinguished but deeply reserved manner, and that during the day he ate nothing but handfuls of toasted millet.

Although Rimbaud seemed briefly to be enjoying himself, soon enough he was back to his old theme in his letters to his mother:

I'm always very bored, in fact, I've never known anyone as bored as I am. And then isn't my existence a miserable one, living as I do without family, without any intellectual stimulation, lost in the midst of niggers [in French, *nègres*] whose lot I'd like to improve but who only seek to exploit you and make it impossible for you to clean up your affairs and get out as quickly as possible? Forced to speak their pidgin and to eat their filthy food, to submit to a thousand inconveniences caused by their laziness, betrayals and stupidity! And that's not even the worst. What's worse still is the fear of slowly becoming as brutish as they are, divorced from all intelligent society.

Rimbaud would openly mock the people of the region or wink behind their backs while looking at another European. But he wasn't merely racist; his misanthropy was general. He despised everyone.

In a letter written to his mother on February 20, 1891, Rimbaud mentions for the first time that he has a terrible pain in his right knee. Once again he blames his suffering on the savages he's living among and the terrible weather and appalling food. He begins to limp. A large tumor develops on his knee. He keeps the leg bandaged, elevated, and massaged—but nothing helps. He can no longer bend his knee and it swells grotesquely.

His mother sends him a jar of salve and two surgical stockings.

Rimbaud knew that in order to receive the proper medical treatment for his knee he needed to get to Marseille, but he kept putting off the trip since he wanted to collect every last penny owed to him. At last he designed a covered litter in which he could ride carried by sixteen hired men over the hills and through the desert. The entire trip to the coast was a long calvary because every jolt shot pain through his entire body. It took his men eleven days to cover the 185 miles from Harar to the port of Zeilah. From there he crossed the Red Sea to Aden, a voyage of three days. In Aden he deposited his currency and got a draft on a French bank. He was then admitted to a hospital there, where the doctor immediately envisaged amputating the long-neglected and tumorous lower leg. But then everyone decided a return trip to France would be best. Rimbaud parted with his tearful servant Djami and boarded the *Amazone* bound for Marseille on May 9, 1891. The trip took eleven days, and on May 20 Rimbaud was admitted to the Hospital of the Conception in Marseille—where he would spend four of the last five months of his life.

The fact that Rimbaud had taken so much time to settle his affairs, first in Harar and then in Aden, weighed against his chances of a cure. He was condemned to death through his own greed. To be sure, his whole destiny was an unhappy one, but he only aggravated his fate by waiting so long to seek treatment.

His leg was finally amputated well above the knee on May 27 by a surgeon, Doctor Édouard Pluyette, who worked under the most modern conditions in a brand-new operating room. Rimbaud was administered chloroform and the room was as sterile as the state of the art permitted. By May he was able to write with confidence to a business associate that within twenty days he would be cured. Rimbaud was already dreaming of returning to Abyssinia and working and getting about normally thanks to an artificial leg. His old boss Alfred Bardey visited him in the hospital and was treated to a long circumstantial account of all his travails in crossing the desert and mountains of Somalia. He learned from Bardey that back in Harar hundreds of thousands of people were dying of famine, and that many had resorted to cannibalism. A drought had destroyed the local grain crops.

By the end of June, Rimbaud was trying to walk with the aid of crutches, but his stump was too painful to support his weight, and the doctors encouraged him to be patient. His mother had come for the operation—it was the first time they'd seen each other in ten years. A visitor, Maurice Riès, was struck by how avaricious and distrustful the Rimbaud family was. A French business associate from Africa, Riès wrote a check for thirty thousand francs to Rimbaud—a sum that was owed to him. A time was set for Riès to accompany Madame Rimbaud to the bank to make the deposit. But, apparently worried that he might rob her on the way, she set off earlier than the appointed time and deposited the check alone. Riès later confessed that he was astonished by this behavior.

Madame Rimbaud left for her farm in the Ardennes just a few days after she had arrived in Marseille, despite Arthur's tears. He began to send letters to his sister alone. On June 23, he wrote: "As for me, all I can do is weep night and day, I'm a dead man, I'm maimed for life. In two weeks I think I'll be cured but I'll never be able to walk without crutches....All my cares are driving me mad. Face it, our life is just one long misery. What are we living for?"

Even with a crutch Arthur could scarcely walk. The cancer and his time in bed had weakened him. Only one bright light shone through the gloom—he discovered that at last his military obligation had been resolved, and he would never have to serve in the army. He made plans to return to the family farm, where he would recuperate, learn to walk with an artificial leg and make ready to return to Africa before the cold weather set in. He wrote Isabelle: "What boredom, what weariness, what sadness when I think of all my former trips and how active I was just five months ago!" Rimbaud's difficulties in walking tormented him, since they spelled his immobility: "Night and day I dwell on my problems of getting around: it's a real torture! I'd like to do this and that, go here and there, look, live, leave: impossible, impossible at least for a long while, if not forever!"

He decided that he'd made a terrible mistake to permit the surgeon to amputate his leg. Anything was better than amputation. Rimbaud's gift for complaining, now that it had a true occasion, became eloquent with grief: "You tremble to see objects and people coming toward you, fear that they might knock you down and break your other leg. People snicker watching you hop about. Even when you're seated again your hands are cramping up, your armpit cut in half, and your face looks idiotic. Despair comes back over you and you stay there seated like a completely useless person, whining and waiting for the night, which will bring constant insomnia and the dawn which will be even sadder than the evening before."

On July 23, after sixty-three days in the hospital, Rimbaud at last caught the train and traveled alone to his mother's farm, changing trains several times. The first few days he was back, he surprised his mother and sister by cracking jokes all the time and reducing them to tears of merriment. He couldn't bear to sit still and went for long rides with them in the horse-drawn open carriage. He'd brought back an Abyssinian harp, which he played in the evenings. But soon enough, a few days later, his morale and his physical state took a downward turn. His armpit ached so much that he couldn't get around on his crutches. He had to sit in a chair or lie in bed all day, and he wept with nervous rage. He remembered that he and his brother as children had once thrown stones at a cripple; now he decided that he was being punished for his childhood sin. His brother, Frédéric, ever since his threat to blackmail Arthur, was banished from the family hearth. No one told him that Arthur was ill and had come home.

Isabelle came to replace his mother in Arthur's affections. It had been relatively easy for Arthur to forget how steely and difficult his mother could be when his only contact with her was epistolary. But now he was living under her roof again and he remembered how tyrannical and unfeeling she could be. Her stoicism rubbed him the wrong way; he preferred his sister's lachrymose devotion. Nor could Arthur forget that his mother had abandoned him in Marseille just a few days after the operation. He had been willing to leave his hard-won little fortune to her, but now he had second thoughts. He no longer loved his mother—and her heart became stony toward him.

Exactly one month to the day after he arrived at the family farm Arthur left on the train with his sister for Marseille again. He was determined to sail for Aden. The trip south was excruciating. Rimbaud was by now in such pain from his cancer—which had spread everywhere—that he sobbed from the movements of the train car. Transferring from one train to another was torture. He declared that the doctors would have to cut off the rest of his wretched leg, so extreme was his pain. Isabelle recalled that in the train he would pile up cushions, shift his position constantly, stand, sit, turn this way and that, but that no matter what position he'd put himself into, the agony was unbearable.

Back in Marseille, Rimbaud was persuaded to return to the hospital. There at least he could receive shots of morphine that eased the pain enough to allow him to sleep at night. But a general paralysis was slowly creeping

over his entire body. His stump—according to Isabelle—
had turned into "an enormous cancer between his hip
and his stomach."

Madame Rimbaud was vexed with her daughter and
son and refused to answer Isabelle's daily letters. The
mother herself was ill and thought Isabelle should be
nursing her and helping her take in the harvest. But, as
Isabelle wrote, Arthur threatened to commit suicide if
she left his side. A new mechanical leg arrived, specially
designed for Arthur, but he said, "I'll never be able
to wear it....It's over, completely over, I feel that I'm
going to die." Since his arms were now paralyzed, the
doctors decided to use a new therapy as a last resort and
to apply electric shock to his limbs—without any success.
Rimbaud's mother was counting on her son's money as
an inheritance and presumably had instructed Isabelle to
ignore his last wishes and to bring home all his worldly
goods. Isabelle staunchly refused: "As for your letter and
Arthur: don't count in any way on his money. After he's
gone and the burial fees are paid and the travel expenses,
etc., you must expect his money will go to other people.
I've absolutely made up my mind to respect his wishes
even though I'm the only one who would execute them,
his money and belongings will go to whomever he sees
fit. What I've done for him I haven't done out of greed,
it's because he's my brother. Even though he's been
abandoned by the entire universe, I haven't wanted to
let him die alone and without help; but I will be loyal to
him in death as in life, and what he tells me to do with his
money and his clothes I will do precisely even if I must

suffer because of it."

Isabelle later recalled that Arthur awoke from a brief nap, looked out the window at the sun and said, "I'm going under the earth and you will walk about in the sunlight." On October 20, 1891, he celebrated his 37th birthday. According to the extremely pious Isabelle, Arthur at this point underwent a deathbed conversion and returned to the Catholic Church. There is no evidence that this "event" was anything more than a fervent wish on the devout sister's part. Rimbaud had been fiercely anticlerical as a poet and later, when he became a more subdued businessman in Africa, he still avoided everything religious. He never attended mass in Harar, even though he was friendly with the French clergy there. Not one word from his pen (unless it is, as Isabelle later claimed, found in obscure passages in *A Season in Hell*) ever hinted at the least belief in God or the mysteries of the Church. Curiously, after this real or false conversion—according to Isabelle—Rimbaud kept invoking Allah.

In his delirium Rimbaud finally felt no more pain. He murmured constantly to Isabelle, often calling her "Djami." In his last moment of consciousness he dictated a letter to the (imaginary) director of a shipping company arranging for his departure. He included an inventory of elephant tusks he wanted to ship. He died on November 10 and his corpse was shipped home, where he was buried with only his mother and sister in attendance. The priest had wanted to notify his old classmates and friends in the region, but Madame Rimbaud had hissed, "Don't make a fuss. It's pointless."

Rimbaud's old piano teacher played the organ. Five choristers sang and eight altar boys were in attendance. Madame Rimbaud paid 82 francs for funeral hangings around the altar and 100 francs for candles. This was an expensive, first-class funeral mass though attended by only two mourners. At last Arthur was buried in the family crypt in the Charleville cemetery with many of his other relatives; here is where hundreds of pilgrims every year come to pay their respects to this troubled soul.

Rimbaud's legend has been amazingly long-lasting, self-contradictory, and widespread, far more vigorous than the posthumous reputation of Verlaine, for instance. Perhaps obscure poets (and Rimbaud invented obscurity) become more renowned than transparent ones since only the obscure need interpretation—that is their lasting appeal both to scholarly exegetes and adolescent mystics. In Rimbaud's case he also had his reputation as a teen rebel going for him—his outrageous arrogance, his photogenic looks, his extreme impertinence, his aberrant sexuality, his definitive renunciation of art at age nineteen and his sudden, bold departure for Africa.

He also had a devoted promoter in Verlaine. To his associates in Harar, Rimbaud spoke of his years with Verlaine either not at all or scornfully. Once Rimbaud told his boss Bardey, who quizzed him about the poets of his past, that he'd known "those birds" rather well; Bardey claimed that Rimbaud once showed him a letter from Verlaine and that Rimbaud said he was sending his old friend a message to "leave me the hell alone!" ("*Foutez-moi le paix!*").

Perhaps Rimbaud knew that people here and there still spoke of them as lovers. Certainly their affair had been notorious, especially after Verlaine was convicted of shooting Rimbaud. If Rimbaud was ashamed of this episode in his life (the drinking, the immorality, his own hooliganism), then no wonder he didn't want to discuss it with the Europeans he was meeting in Africa. He wanted to prove to them his trustworthiness and upstanding character.

Verlaine, despite the lack of contact with Rimbaud, remained faithful to his genius. In 1883 he published three pamphlets called *The Accursed Poets* (*Les Poètes Maudits*) about Rimbaud, Mallarmé, and Tristan Corbière. All three, now recognized as among the giants of their day, were unknown when Verlaine decided to write about them. The text dedicated to Rimbaud was especially courageous since it might have dredged up the scandals of the past: the trial, the imprisonment, his immoral relations with Rimbaud, the divorce. Bitter and angry and derisive toward Rimbaud in the years 1875 to 1880, Verlaine now spoke of him only with affection and admiration. In the pamphlet Verlaine reproduced several of Rimbaud's poems, which many people in literary Paris were reading for the first time. They were stunned. As Edmond Lepelletier wrote, no one had very favorable memories of the boy they'd met fifteen years before. All they recalled were his beastly manners and the high opinion he had of himself: "The quotations that Verlaine gave were like a revelation." Without Verlaine's efforts Rimbaud would be just a footnote in the history of a forgotten literary movement, *Zutisme*.

Three years later, in 1886, the *Illuminations* were published for the first time—initially in a literary journal,

La Vogue, and then in book form. If their publication was delayed so long, it was because the manuscript had fallen into the hands of Mathilde, Verlaine's wife, who was determined to do nothing to promote the reputation of her old rival. But once her divorce went through and she remarried and was no longer stigmatized by Verlaine's name, she relented and surrendered the manuscript. The prose poems appeared in five successive numbers of the review. The book came out in 1886 in an edition of two hundred copies, with a biographical note by Verlaine. *La Vogue* then followed up its success by reprinting in three issues all of *A Season in Hell*.

Although the number of copies may sound small, they had a big impact on other writers. The young Paul Claudel, who would later become one of Rimbaud's most ardent champions, was stunned by the works he read in *La Vogue*. He claimed that he'd felt "a living and nearly physical impression of the supernatural" while reading *A Season in Hell*.

While Rimbaud was still alive and working in Africa, rumors about him circulated wildly in France. Some people claimed he was creating works of art in Asia. Others said he was in Africa where he was the "king of the niggers" (*roi de nègres*). Still others insisted he was a pig farmer somewhere or a murderous peasant (*un paysan assassin*). Only one literary journal, *Le Symboliste*, gave accurate information about his whereabouts and activities and even included an interview with Rimbaud's erstwhile boss Alfred Bardey.

In 1887 a false report of Rimbaud's death made the rounds in Paris and inspired Verlaine to write one of his greatest poems, "*Laeti et errabundi*," in which he exclaims:

> They say you're dead—you! May the devil
> Take him, whoever is spreading
> This irreparable rumor
> Clamoring at my door!
>
> I don't want to believe it. Dead, you,
> My little one, full god among the half-gods!
> Those who are saying it are crazy—
> Why, dead, my great radiant sin,
>
> You, the miracle-working poem
> And my all-knowing philosophy,
> And my homeland and my bohemia,
> All dead? Well, then, live my life!

Although Verlaine published many poems written to the various men and women in his life, nothing ever equaled the passion and intensity of this tribute to a man he hadn't seen in fifteen years.

In 1888 Verlaine published *Arthur Rimbaud* in a series called "Men of Today." Most of the biographical information in it was inaccurate or evasive. According to Verlaine, Rimbaud was alive and well and living in Aden where he was engaged in creating, for his own pleasure, gigantic works of art. Again, Verlaine quoted extensively from Rimbaud's poems—especially the sonnet "Vowels," which had almost instantly become an anthology piece. By this point Rimbaud had become so celebrated that other poets were writing fakes—which Verlaine took pains to unmask and denounce.

Rimbaud was now considered one of the leaders not only of the Symbolists but also of the Decadents (a movement he no doubt had never heard of). The editor of a small literary journal in Marseille had written Rimbaud in care of the French consul in Aden on July 17, 1890, asking him for some new verses and declaring his admiration. Rimbaud did not respond.

After his death in 1891, his sister Isabelle began to write frequently about Arthur. She wanted everyone to regard him as a saint and she made a great point of stressing his deathbed conversion and his angelic kindness to his colleagues and servants in Africa. Isabelle married an ambitious writer who'd given himself the name of Paterne Berrichon; although he'd never met Rimbaud he was soon producing portraits of the dead poet and writing eulogies to his genius and his saintliness.

Soon almost every cause and school and movement, serious or frivolous, popular or classical, was embracing Rimbaud. At one extreme were the Catholics, led by Isabelle Rimbaud and Paul Claudel, the great religious poet and playwright (*The Annunciation Made to Mary*). At the other extreme were the Surrealists who, starting in the 1920s, declared Rimbaud one of their formative influences and precursors. By 1961 a two-volume work in French had been published called *The Myth of Rimbaud* (*Le mythe de Rimbaud*). Just a glance at the index reveals that a virtual library of theses and scholarly articles and critical books had already been devoted to Rimbaud the Symbolist, Rimbaud the Decadent, Rimbaud the Surrealist, Rimbaud the Cabbalist, Rimbaud the Magician, Rimbaud the Saint, Rimbaud the Fascist, Rimbaud the French patriot, Rimbaud the Communard, Rimbaud the Bolshevist, Rimbaud the Honest Bourgeois, Rimbaud the Voice of the Ardennes, Rimbaud the Man of Action, Rimbaud the Adventurer, Rimbaud the Thug, and Rimbaud the Pervert!

Everyone has now weighed in on Rimbaud. Marcel Proust wrote that he was "almost superhuman." Bob Dylan in a song lyric said, "Relationships have all been bad, mine have been like Verlaine's and Rimbaud's" (from "You're Going to Make Me Lonesome When You Go"). Patti Smith wrote a song called "Easter" about Rimbaud's first communion. Jim Morrison claimed Rimbaud as his "master." Antonin Artaud announced that Rimbaud had been killed "because they wanted to kill him." (The "they" was never made clear.) Milan Kundera wrote that in 1968 "thousands of Rimbauds" took to the barricades in the worldwide student rebellions. Jack Kerouac wrote a poem to Rimbaud—in fact all the Beats honored the man who had called for a systematic disordering of the senses. Roland Barthes analyzed him, as did Sartre, who dissected the statement "*Je est un autre*"—"I is someone else"—and contrasted him (favorably) to Baudelaire. Martin Heidegger, Mario Vargas Llosa, Pablo Neruda, Jean Cocteau, Lawrence Durrell—every important thinker and artist of the last hundred years has had an opinion about Rimbaud, who continues to elude us as he streaks just ahead of our grasp on his "soles of wind" (*semelles de vent*).

Bibliography

The best biography in French of Rimbaud is *Arthur Rimbaud* by Jean-Jacques Lefrère, which is 1,242 pages long. Published by Fayard in 2001, it is a remarkable piece of sober and detailed research and analysis, a true monument to its subject, neither a hagiography nor a pathography. In 2008 Lefrère also published the complete letters, 1,032 pages long, *Arthur Rimbaud: Correspondance*. There are many other earlier excellent and readable biographies in French, including several that have been translated into English. The best are *Arthur Rimbaud: Presence of an Enigma* by Jean-Luc Steinmetz, *Rimbaud* by Pierre Petitfils, and (in French only) *La vie de Rimbaud* by André Dhotel and *Rimbaud* by Claude Jeancolas.

In English the classic biography is Enid Starkie's *Rimbaud*, originally published in 1937. Starkie writes like a novelist and some of her conclusions are more fictional than factual. Of contemporary biographies in English, Graham Robb's *Rimbaud* is by far the best, and I am heavily indebted to it. There are two important books about Rimbaud in Africa: *Rimbaud in Abyssinia* by Alain Borer, and *Somebody Else: Arthur Rimbaud in*

Africa by Charles Nicholl. Steve Murphy (in spite of his name) writes in French and is the author of *Rimbaud et la menagerie impériale*, about Rimbaud and the Second Empire, as well as *Le Premier Rimbaud ou l'apprentissage de la subversion*. The now old but still informative and useful guide to Rimbaud's posthumous "career" is René Étiemble's *Le Mythe de Rimbaud*.

In French the most accurate and complete biography of Verlaine is Alain Buisine's *Verlaine: Histoire d'un corps*. In English there are several older biographies. The best one is *Verlaine* by Joanna Richardson. The classic biography is Henri Troyat's *Verlaine*. Lawrence and Elisabeth Hanson wrote *Verlaine: Prince of Poets* (in America titled *Verlaine: Fool of God*), which manages to sidestep the question of his homosexuality—a rather grave omission.

I consulted a biography of Rimbaud's mother, *Madame Rimbaud*, by Françoise Lalande, and I devoured a thesis on Germain Nouveau by Alexandre L. Amprimoz.

Of course there were many books written by Rimbaud's relatives and friends, including those by his teacher, Georges Izambard, his sister Isabelle and her husband, Paterne Berrichon, his childhood friend Ernest Delahaye and many others, but most of these books are out of print and of interest only to specialists. Paul Claudel's preface to Rimbaud's complete works dates from a 1912 edition and should be read as an eloquent if nearly indefensible position on the great poet. At the other extreme is the entry on Rimbaud in an anthology of black humor by the "pope of surrealism," André Breton (Breton faults Rimbaud for being insufficiently comic).

For Rimbaud's poetry, I am indebted to Alain Borer's centenary edition, *Oeuvre-Vie*, which presents the work exactly in the order it was written and without any later added apparatus. The standard edition of the *Oeuvres complètes* is the 1972 Pléiade edited by Antoine Adam; its annotations are invaluable both as history and interpretation. In English there are several complete translations of the poetry. Wallace Fowlie's *Rimbaud: Complete Works, Selected Letters*—a bilingual edition revised by Seth Whidden—is useful though not as accurate as the Penguin *Arthur Rimbaud: Selected Poems and Letters*, translated and annotated by Jeremy Harding and John Sturrock. Wyatt Mason has translated the complete letters in a Modern Library edition. The best translation of a single work is Alan Jenkins' Englishing of "The Drunken Boat." In my biography all the translations from Rimbaud and Verlaine are mine.

For Verlaine there is a Pléiade of his complete prose and another of his complete poetry. In addition Gallimard has published a comprehensive *Album Rimbaud*, which gives most of the extant images of Rimbaud and his world, and a less satisfying *Album Verlaine*.

In English there are so many critical studies that one doesn't know where to begin. Perhaps the best known are Henry Miller's *The Time of the Assassins*, Wallace Fowlie's *Rimbaud*, and Edmund Wilson's study of symbolism, *Axel's Castle*.

Probably most people today have encountered Rimbaud and Verlaine through the Leonardo DiCaprio film *Total Eclipse*.

Acknowledgments

I'd like to thank Michael Carroll for once again taking out time from his own writing to help prepare and proofread this text. His encouragement, advice, and loyalty are priceless. I trust his judgment absolutely and am grateful for his impeccable ear for language and sharp eye for consistency.

This book is dedicated to Carol Rigolot, my colleague at Princeton who has always inspired me with her warmth and intelligence and indefatigable energy. We are comrades at arms in the sometimes fraught world of French scholarship in America.

I'd like to thanks James Atlas for commissioning this biography—it joins the brief life of Proust I wrote as the first volume in his now extensive collection. Amanda Urban, my agent, is my best reader and always the ideal representative.

My friend Elisabeth Ladenson has always been encouraging to me—she is someone with whom I love to talk about French literature and whose erudition and eloquence I so much admire. She introduced me to Antoine Compagnon, who gave me some invaluable leads in researching this book. Marie-Madeleine Rigopoulos also helped me more than she might have suspected. Claude Arnaud, the great biographer of Cocteau, gave me permission to pursue some of my odd hunches about Rimbaud. Another biographer, Kirk Davis Swinehart, did me the honor of listening to pages in progress and demonstrating his enthusiasm for the way I was going about my project.

Joyce Carol Oates has accompanied me along the sometimes thorny way of writing this little book, as she has so often in the past.